Failed Relations

Studies in Feminist Philosophy is designed to showcase cutting-edge monographs and collections that display the full range of feminist approaches to philosophy, that push feminist thought in important new directions, and that display the outstanding quality of feminist philosophical thought.

STUDIES IN FEMINIST PHILOSOPHY

Elizabeth Barnes, University of Virginia
Elizabeth Brake, Rice University
Kristie Dotson, University of Michigan
Miranda Fricker, NYU
Ann Garry, California State University, Los Angeles
Sally Haslanger, MIT
Alison Jaggar, University of Colorado, Boulder
Serene Khader, CUNY Graduate Center

Jennifer Mcweeny, Emerson College
Mari Mikkola, Universiteit van Amsterdam
Sarah Clark Miller, Penn State University
Andrea Pitts, University of Buffalo
Jennifer Saul, University of Waterloo
Lisa Tessman, Binghamton University
Nancy Tuana, Penn State University

Published in the Series:

Gender in the Mirror: Cultural Imagery & Women's Agency
Diana Tietjens Meyers

Autonomy, Gender, Politics
Marilyn Friedman

Abortion and Social Responsibility: Depolarizing the Debate
Laurie Shrage

Setting the Moral Compass: Essays by Women Philosophers
Edited by Cheshire Calhoun

On Female Body Experience: "Throwing Like a Girl" and Other Essays
Iris Marion Young

Burdened Virtues: Virtue Ethics for Liberatory Struggles
Lisa Tessman

Women and Citizenship
Edited by Marilyn Friedman

Visible Identities: Race, Gender and the Self
Linda Martín Alcoff

Analyzing Oppression
Anne E. Cudd

Ecological Thinking: The Politics of Epistemic Location
Lorraine Code

Women's Liberation and the Sublime: Feminism, Postmodernism, Environment
Bonnie Mann

Family Bonds: Genealogies of Race and Gender
Ellen K. Feder

Self Transformations: Foucault, Ethics, and Normalized Bodies
Cressida J. Heyes

Moral Understandings: A Feminist Study in Ethics, Second Edition
Margaret Urban Walker

The Moral Skeptic
Anita M. Superson

"You've Changed": Sex Reassignment and Personal Identity
Edited by Laurie J. Shrage

Dancing with Iris: The Philosophy of Iris Marion Young
Edited by Ann Ferguson and Mechthild Nagel

Philosophy of Science after Feminism
Janet A. Kourany

Shifting Ground: Knowledge and Reality, Transgression and Trustworthiness
Naomi Scheman

Adaptive Preferences and Women's Empowerment
Serene Khader

The Metaphysics of Gender
Charlotte Witt

Unpopular Privacy: What Must We Hide?
Anita L. Allen

Out from the Shadows: Analytic Feminist Contributions to Traditional Philosophy
Edited by Sharon L. Crasnow and Anita M. Superson

Minimizing Marriage: Marriage, Morality, and the Law
Elizabeth Brake

Simone de Beauvoir and the Politics of Ambiguity
Sonia Kruks

The Epistemology of Resistance: Gender and Racial Oppression, Epistemic Injustice, and Resistant Imaginations
José Medina

Identities and Freedom: Feminist Theory between Power and Connection
Allison Weir

Vulnerability: New Essays in Ethics and Feminist Philosophy
Edited by Catriona Mackenzie, Wendy Rogers, and Susan Dodds

Sovereign Masculinity: Gender Lessons from the War on Terror
Bonnie Mann

Our Faithfulness to the Past: Essays on the Ethics and Politics of Memory
Sue Campbell, edited by Christine M. Koggel and Rockney Jacobsen

Autonomy, Oppression, and Gender
Edited by Andrea Veltman and Mark Piper

The Physiology of Sexist and Racist Oppression
Shannon Sullivan

Disorientation and Moral Life
Ami Harbin

The Minority Body: A Theory of Disability
Elizabeth Barnes

The Wrong of Injustice: Dehumanization and Its Role in Feminist Philosophy
Mari Mikkola

Beyond Speech: Pornography and Analytic Feminist Philosophy
Mari Mikkola

Differences: Rereading Beauvoir and Irigaray
Edited by Emily Anne Parker and Anne van Leeuwen

Categories We Live By
Ásta

Equal Citizenship and Public Reason
Christie Hartley and Lori Watson

Decolonizing Universalism: A Transnational Feminist Ethic
Serene J. Khader

Women's Activism, Feminism, and Social Justice
Margaret A. McLaren

Theories of the Flesh: Latinx and Latin American Feminisms, Transformation, and Resistance
Edited by Andrea J. Pitts, Mariana Ortega, and José Medina

Elemental Difference and the Climate of the Body
Emily Anne Parker

Being Born: Birth and Philosophy
Alison Stone

Hope Under Oppression
Katie Stockdale

Racial Climates, Ecological Indifference: An Ecointersectional Approach
Nancy Tuana

The Epistemology of Protest: Silencing, Epistemic Activism, and the Communicative Life of Resistance
José Medina

Ontology and Oppression: Race, Gender, and Social Reality
Katharine Jenkins

On Taking Offence
Emily McTernan

Nonideal Theory and Content Externalism
Jeff Engelhardt

Decolonizing Freedom
Allison Weir

Global Sweatshops: A Feminist Theory of Exploitation and Resistance
Mirjam Müller

The Dynamics of Epistemic Injustice: Situating Epistemic Power and Agency
Amandine Catala

Stereotypes and Scripts
Samia Hesni

Failed Relations: Oppression and Relational Autonomy
Rebekah Johnston

Failed Relations

Oppression and Relational Autonomy

REBEKAH JOHNSTON

OXFORD
UNIVERSITY PRESS

Oxford University Press is a department of the University of Oxford.
It furthers the University's objective of excellence in research, scholarship,
and education by publishing worldwide. Oxford is a registered trade mark of
Oxford University Press in the UK and certain other countries.

Published in the United States of America by Oxford University Press
198 Madison Avenue, New York, NY 10016, United States of America.

© Oxford University Press 2025

All rights reserved. No part of this publication may be reproduced, stored in a retrieval system, transmitted, used for text and data mining, or used for training artificial intelligence, in any form or by any means, without the prior permission in writing of Oxford University Press, or as expressly permitted by law, by license or under terms agreed with the appropriate reprographics rights organization. Inquiries concerning reproduction outside the scope of the above should be sent to the Rights Department, Oxford University Press, at the address above.

You must not circulate this work in any other form
and you must impose this same condition on any acquirer.

CIP data is on file at the Library of Congress

ISBN 978-0-19-779577-4 (pbk.)
ISBN 978-0-19-779576-7 (hbk.)

DOI: 10.1093/oso/9780197795767.001.0001

Paperback printed by Marquis Book Printing, Canada
Hardback printed by Bridgeport National Bindery, Inc., United States of America

The manufacturer's authorized representative in the EU for product safety is
Oxford University Press España S.A., Parque Empresarial San Fernando de Henares,
Avenida de Castilla, 2 – 28830 Madrid (www.oup.es/en).

For Allison and Carol and JJ and Kathryn

Contents

Acknowledgments — xi

Introduction — 1

1. Living with Who Others Get to Be: Self-Determination and Status — 15

2. Self-Governance, Self-Expressive Activities, and Communal Competence — 33

3. Self-Governance, Hermeneutical Resources, and Communicative Needs — 60

4. Authenticity and Constitutively Relational Emotions — 83

5. Self-Authorization and Social Recognition — 100

Conclusion — 121

References — 137
Index — 141

Acknowledgments

This book unfolded over the course of several years, and it is a pleasure to have an opportunity to express my gratitude for the many people who supported me and this project.

I wish especially to thank Diana Meyers, Paul Benson, and Catriona Mackenzie for their astute and nuanced comments on the entire manuscript. I deeply appreciate their time, intellectual energy, and careful engagement with this work. Thank you also to the editors at Oxford; the series editor, Cheshire Calhoun, for the valuable direction, and Lucy Randall and Zara Cannon-Mohammed for their guidance and excellent work throughout this process.

For making a wonderful place to teach and do philosophy, for their support, and for their intellectual engagement and companionship, I thank my friends and colleagues in the Philosophy Department at Wilfrid Laurier University: Kathy Behrendt, Neil Campbell, Renato Cristi, Gary Foster, Rockney Jacobsen, Jill Rusin, Byron Williston, and the late James Wong. I especially wish to thank Ashwani Peetush for his creative practices of solidarity and playful terms of endearment and Christinia Landry for her wry humor and for always knowing the appropriate amount of everything. For their contributions to sustaining the daily life of our department, I wish to thank Jane Osborne, Kristine Dyck, and Andrea Nechita.

Many graduate students have given their time and intellectual energy to engaging this project. I owe a particular debt of gratitude to the members of our 2021–2022 and 2022–2023 graduate cohorts, Logan Clendenning, Eric Duvall, Kawthar Fedjki, Regina Fidelis Iligan, Deja Mckennon, Aaron Ricard, Rayanna de Faria Calaza Rocha, Ajmal Roshan, Janakhan Sivapalasingam, David Smenderovac, Pragya Upreti, and Nicole Walker, for their engagement with several draft chapters of this book. Thanks is due also to Katherine Bourdeau, Sarah Corbett, Pamela Dedman, Janet Kwon, Evan Mackie, Megan McDonald, Joan Mulholland, and Nicole Ramsoomair for the many helpful conversations.

I am grateful to the many undergraduate students I've had the pleasure to teach over the years and especially to Dana Arafa, Julia Chiavegato, and

Antonio Rodriguez for their astute and often humorous engagement with this project and for being fabulous and insightful humans.

I benefited greatly from brief and more extended conversations at several workshops and conferences. Thank you to Nabina Liebow, Marina Oshana, Christian Schemmel, Muhammad Velji, Kristin Voigt, and Andrea Westlund. I especially wish to thank Natalie Stoljar for her insightful engagement and for welcoming me into the community of scholars working in this area when I first started work on this project.

I am grateful for the many people over the years who have sustained me and enriched my life. I owe a particular debt of gratitude to Marguerite Deslauriers for her excellent mentorship, intellectual engagement, and friendship over many years. I am thankful to the following people who have engaged me in many valued ways: Monique Biggs, for her love, her warmth and support, and especially for her creative listening practices that not only keep me laughing but also allow me to expand in surprising ways; Allauren Forbes, a former student and now valued colleague and friend, for her generous engagement with this project over the course of many years; Angela Garcia, for the COVID letters; Julie Johnson, for being a constant champion of the project and a valued source of humor, insight, warmth, and friendship; Lisa Young Kutsukake, my poet, for her generosity of spirit, for sharing her expansive ways of thinking, and for all the forms our letters take; Kara Richardson, for the many lovely early years in which we learned to do philosophy together; Sarah Martineau, for the red-pen corrections and occasional allowances; Rayne Rose, for the many beautiful things we made; Kyle Shellington, for his impeccably executed sarcasm; Mitchell Solsky, for sharing his 'prettiest bird' energy; and, my friend and colleague, Margaret Toye, for the picnics, the sustaining correspondence, and her encouraging and nuanced engagement with this work. Thank you also to Sara Bannerman, Sara Clay, Suzanne Lazrado, Cecelia Sparrow, and Lorraine Wilson.

I am grateful to my family for their generous love and support. I thank my parents, Dan and Bev Johnston, for their ongoing love and care. Thank you to my siblings, Angela Johnston, Naomi Johnston, and Tim Johnston, for their humor, their teasing, the music, and for always making me feel at home with them. Thank you also to Madilyn Johnston, Wesley Johnston, Jessica Johnston, Mark Ireland, Ken Theal, my grandparents Maurice (Mike) and Diana Johnston, and my late grandparents Anita Fidler, Douglas Fidler, and Fern Johnston. Thank you to Joyce Hendy, Ron Taylor, Peter Taylor, and Jinkx Taylor for making me a part of the family.

This book is dedicated to those who have sustained me over many years and without whom I could not have written this book. My dear friend and colleague Allison Weir has been a constant source of intellectual and creative engagement, and I thank her especially for the humor with which she enacts and sustains our many ways of being together—and for all the metaphorical limo rides. Thank you to my cousin, Carol Theal, for the many years of Mathes humor, for always believing in me, for keeping the chandelier shined, and especially for "seeing me first." Thank you to my dear friend, JJ Dinishak, for helping me to work out the initial idea for this book, for the many years of solidarity, for being my partner in many adventures, and for keeping me close despite our geographical distance.

Finally, I am forever thankful to Kathryn Taylor for their enduring love, engagement, and support. I am grateful to them for the many conversations about this book, for the joy they bring to my life, for their enlivening and delightful wit, and for always letting me sit with them.

Introduction

> Facing, confronting, branding each other
> We were made through one another
> Great expectations, great expectations, great expectations.
> —Cat Power, "Great Expectations"

> Freedom, then, is an ongoing practice of finding and creating and affirming as well as questioning and criticising our identities, which are our connections. Once practices of freedom are understood to be renegotiations of our connections, then practices of freedom can be compatible with the practice of a meaningful life lived with others: a practice of interdependence, or social freedom.
> —Allison Weir, *Identities and Freedom*

As vulnerable living beings, beings with bodily, emotional, and intellectual needs for sustenance, creativity, and connection, we all inevitably depend on relations with others. The relations in which we stand—with other people, with institutions, and with physical, social, emotional, and intellectual resources—have profound effects on who we can be and the lives we can live. My aim in this book is to articulate some of the multifaceted and often subtle layers of relationality that are significant to the achievement and maintenance of personal autonomy.

At a general level, theories of personal autonomy are theories that seek to specify the conditions that must be met in order for a person's life, identity, desires, motivations, values, and actions truly to count as her own. Achieving and maintaining personal autonomy involves rational, imaginative, creative, and aesthetic capacities and, in its contemporary iterations, as I outline below, is thoroughly social. To make one's life one's own, in the senses relevant to personal autonomy, is not to escape relation; autonomy is deeply and intricately dependent on relations of many sorts. In this book, I identify some of the ways in which oppressive social circumstances constrain the autonomy of marginalized people by actively failing to provide and sustain the relations required for autonomy.

Identifying these failures of relation provides a ground for social critique. Personal autonomy is a central value of liberal democracies. Articulating the ways in which social systems and the relations they support or constrain matter to autonomy, therefore, provides specific grounds from which to critique those structures and insight into what relations to work toward in seeking social change. As Veltman and Piper point out, "Insofar as liberal democracies value individual autonomy, ideals of autonomy provide norms for critiquing oppressive practices that stifle agency and limit opportunities" (2014, 2). Tracing impediments to autonomy caused by oppressive, exploitative, and marginalizing social conditions provides us with specific reasons for objecting to such social practices and with a clear articulation of what changes are necessary to furnish a more adequate social infrastructure.

My starting point is not to defend the value of the concept of autonomy for feminist and other liberatory movements. While the value of the concept of personal autonomy for feminist theory has a contentious history, Mackenzie and Stoljar (2000) and Friedman (2003) have provided compelling arguments for its importance to understanding and addressing oppression. I adopt Mackenzie and Stoljar's refiguration of the concept as thoroughly relational. In their seminal 2000 collection, *Relational Autonomy: Feminist Perspectives on Autonomy, Agency, and the Social Self*, they address the charge that "the concept of autonomy is inherently masculinist, that it is inextricably bound up with masculine character ideals, with assumptions about selfhood and agency that are metaphysically, epistemologically, and ethically problematic from a feminist perspective" (2000, 3). While admitting the aptness of these critiques in relation to some conceptions of autonomy, Mackenzie and Stoljar defend the claim that "the notion of autonomy is vital to feminist attempts to understand oppression, subjection, and agency" (3). Given its central importance, they "reconceptualise and refigure the concept of individual autonomy from a feminist perspective" (4). This refiguration is what they call "relational autonomy."

"Relational autonomy" does not pick out a "unified conception of autonomy but is rather an umbrella term, designating a range of related perspectives" (Mackenzie and Stoljar 2000, 4). What relates the perspectives that fall under the umbrella term "relational autonomy" is "a shared conviction, the conviction that persons are socially embedded and that agents' identities are formed within the context of social relationships and shaped by a complex of intersecting social determinants such as race, class, gender, and ethnicity" (4). My project is firmly grounded in this refigured conception of autonomy.

Since the publication of this volume, there has been a proliferation of insightful and valuable work outlining connections between oppression and the diminishment of autonomy. These accounts of relational autonomy can be broadly divided into causally relational and constitutively relational accounts.[1] Causally relational theories typically focus on the inner psychological lives of agents and the causal interplay between internal life and the external features of one's environment. On causally relational views, social relations causally contribute to inner life in ways that either enable or impede autonomy. For example, socialization to feminine gender roles may cause an agent to undervalue her own ambitions or overvalue the role of physical beauty. Or pervasive denigrating treatment of members of marginalized groups may cause an erosion of the self-respect, self-worth, and self-esteem needed to be autonomous. Constitutively relational views focus more directly on social relations and are committed to the claim that "[a]utonomy is a condition of persons constituted in large part by the social relations people find themselves in and by the absence of other social relations" (Oshana 2006, 49). On constitutively relational accounts, social relations can constitute one as autonomous or not. For example, being imprisoned or economically exploited may diminish one's practical control over one's life in ways that *constitute* constraints on autonomy. On constitutively relational views "[a]utonomy is not a phenomenon merely enhanced or lessened by the contingencies of a person's social situation; social relations do not just causally facilitate or impair the exercise of autonomy. Rather, appropriate social relations form an inherent part of what it means be self-directed" (49).

With the notable exception of Marina Oshana's (2006) work, the vast majority of accounts give causally relational treatments of the connections between social relations and autonomy and center for analysis the autonomy-diminishing results of internalized oppression. While this work is extremely valuable, it is, in my view, too narrow fully to capture the ways in which oppressive social circumstances constrain autonomy. My goal in this book is to provide a richer articulation of the relationship between social relations and

---

[1] It is important to note that a single theory can combine causally relational and constitutively relational accounts. This will be further elaborated in chapter 1.

autonomy by focusing on constituting relations. Some of these constituting relations are straightforwardly about the external relations in which we stand and how they constrain agents in terms of their freedoms and opportunities. Others identify constitutively relational aspects of autonomy that depend on relations with others to constitute aspects of the inner life of an agent. One of my central goals is to trouble the idea that oppression matters to the inner lives of agents primarily or exclusively through a causal model. Social circumstances can also affect the inner lives of agents by failing to provide the constituting relations necessary for autonomy. I identify several ways in which social relations impede autonomy, not by causing damage to the inner lives of agents through, for example, the internalization of oppressive norms, but through failures of co-constitution necessary for autonomy. In other words, I track the ways in which failures of relation matter to autonomy because they withhold constituting elements of autonomy or of the resources needed for autonomy.

In order to bring into focus these constitutively relational aspects of and supporting conditions for autonomy, I move away from an analysis of internalized oppression in order to engage a different range of examples. Causally relational accounts are primarily focused on articulating the ways in which oppression, often through the internalization of oppressive norms, damages agents. This is important, but an exclusive focus on the ways in which oppression damages the inner lives or psychologies of marginalized agents generates a dichotomous interpretive lens. On these models, one must either accept that oppressive structures of racism, sexism, heterosexism, and so on impede autonomy by *damaging* the psychology of an agent or that oppressive structures are irrelevant to assessments of autonomy. In my view, many of the ordinary, everyday experiences that mark the lives of members of marginalized groups make clear that oppressive social structures impede one's ability to make one's life one's own. But I do not think that adopting a story of "inner" damage through the internalization of false norms, norms that distort values or erode capacities or undermine self-evaluative attitudes, always accurately describes the ways in which oppression matters to autonomy. While agents cannot simply resist this kind of damage alone, agents are often embedded in caring communities that offset these kinds of internal damage. My focus, therefore, is on articulating relations between autonomy and oppressive social circumstances in cases where agents do not internalize oppressive, damaging norms and values.

As a way to clarify and articulate the range of ways in which oppressive social circumstances matter to autonomy in excess of models based on damage, I move away from a focus on socialization and center for analysis examples that engage experiences of living among those empowered to harass others, of epistemic injustice, of co-constituted affect, and of queer orientations in the world. My engagement with examples that are not primarily focused on socialization provides material that seeks, not to dispute the insights of causally relational views, but to suggest that there are additional ways in which oppressive social relations matter to autonomy. My goal in this book is not to propose and defend a full view of autonomy nor to propose necessary and sufficient conditions for autonomy, but to articulate some of the constitutively relational constraints on autonomy that arise from failures of relation in oppressive social contexts.

The book is structured around Mackenzie's insight that "autonomy is a multidimensional, rather than a unitary concept" (2014, 15). Unitary concepts are concepts "for which there is a single set of necessary and sufficient conditions for the correct application of the concept. Natural kind terms such as water, gold, and elephant are unitary concepts" (16). Mackenzie also notes that "[e]thical concepts such as goodness, trust, and autonomy, are also often treated as unitary concepts" (16). Mackenzie, however, argues that autonomy should instead be taken as a multidimensional concept. Autonomy, when taken as a unitary concept, is typically grounded in "the unitary concept of self-governance, the idea that to be autonomous is to be capable of making decisions and acting on the basis of motives, values, or reasons that are 'one's own' in some relevant sense" (16–17). Discussions of autonomy as self-governance typically focus on specifying competence and authenticity conditions, and debate between theorists has "focused on advancing differing interpretations of these conditions, with debate proceeding by way of examples and counterexamples designed to test the necessity or sufficiency claims of rival interpretations" (17). Mackenzie notes that "no agreement on a single definitive interpretation of the competence or authenticity conditions for autonomy has emerged from the debate" and suggests that this is because autonomy is not in fact a unitary concept (17). A multidimensional concept is needed because "the concept of autonomy is employed for different purposes in different social and normative contexts" (16). While all the different employments of the concept track, in significant respects, the ways in which and the degrees to which agents make their lives their own, the multiple factors actually being tracked, in many cases, are not commensurable and thus are not comparable on a signal scale. For example, consider two agents who both value being a voice for change on behalf of their respective communities. Both agents, if they are truly to be autonomous by living according to their own values, must enact this value (to some degree) in their lives. Imagine, however, that both agents very rarely manage to enact this value in their lives. Our first agent very rarely speaks up on behalf of her community because she very rarely has the opportunity to do so; she is excluded from contexts of power where important decisions are made, either outright or through practical barriers such as her rural location, and she has no access to platforms from which her voice can be heard. Our second agent also very rarely speaks up on behalf of her community despite having opportunities to do so. She has platforms from which her voice can be heard, but she rarely makes use of them because she is frequently distracted by immediate pleasures which she pursues instead. Both of these agents suffer a diminishment of autonomy, yet the diminishments are not articulable on a single evaluative scale. The degree to which our first agent's autonomy is compromised is not directly comparable with the degree to which our second agent's autonomy is compromised. Adopting a multidimensional concept of autonomy allows us to recognize that we are tracking autonomy in both cases, without requiring direct commensurability of the specifics of the autonomy-diminishing elements of each example.

Let me clarify some of the specifics of Mackenzie's proposal. As a multidimensional concept, autonomy has several different aspects or axes. For Mackenzie, "the concept of autonomy involves three distinct but causally interdependent dimensions or axes: self-determination, self-governance, and self-authorization" (2014, 17). On Mackenzie's view, "[s]elf-determination involves having the freedom and opportunities to make and enact choices of practical import to one's life, that is, choices about what to value, who to be, and what to do" (17). These freedoms and opportunities include, for example, freedom safely to navigate one's social world and freedom from capricious interference with one's plans, as well as opportunities to access education, adequate housing, and meaningful work. Self-governance "involves having the skills and capacities necessary to make choices and enact decisions that express, or cohere with, one's reflectively constituted diachronic practical identity" (17). A self-governing agent engages in complex practices of self-definition; she participates in the fashioning of who she is through the adoption of values that structure her motivational orientations and also attempts to express herself and her values through her conduct. Finally, "*self-authorization*, involves regarding oneself as having the *normative authority* to be self-determining and self-governing. In other words, it involves regarding oneself as authorized to exercise practical control over one's life, to determine one's own reasons for action, and to define one's values and identity-shaping commitments" (18). Self-authorizing agents actively occupy a position of authority as answerable for who they are and what they do. Each axis identifies distinct but interrelated aspects of personal autonomy, and each "[d]imension involves distinct conditions, which may be satisfied to varying degrees" (15–16).

Adopting this multidimensional concept of autonomy is especially productive for articulating the insights generated by conflicting intuitions about autonomy. While many theorists try to think through these conflicting intuitions about autonomy under a unitary conception of autonomy as self-governance, Mackenzie suggests that "many of the examples and counterexamples in the literature on relational autonomy appeal to these conflicting intuitions and that the unitary concept of self-governance is inadequate to account for them" (2014, 40). The conflicting intuitions often focus on tensions that arise from attempting to account for the important social and political dimensions of autonomy, the structural systems in which one finds oneself, and the "inner" governing structures a person applies or fails to apply in her life. For example, consider an agent who faces severely restrictive oppressive social constraints on the freedoms and opportunities he enjoys in his social context, yet who consistently lives according to values he has fashioned for himself from within those confines. On the one hand, intuitions draw attention to the ways in which this agent is constrained by the social and political conditions in which he lives. On the other hand, intuitions draw attention to the ways in which this person remains central in determining and living up to his own values. To take another example, an agent may enjoy many enabling opportunities and freedoms yet nevertheless lack an adequate sense of herself, her values, and her responsibility to live her life according to her own sense of what is important. Again our intuitions are likely drawn in conflicting directions. This agent seems to enjoy a lack of constraint yet struggles to generate her own reasons and live up to her own values. Moreover, attempts to compare the level of autonomy each of these two agents enjoys also generates conflicting intuitions. The agent in the second example seems to enjoy a lack of constraint that implies a higher degree of autonomy than the person in the first example. Yet the agent in the first example appears to have a relation to himself that points to his having a higher degree of autonomy than the person in the second example.

Mackenzie's multidimensional concept of autonomy allows room to give weight to these conflicting intuitions. She argues that "distinguishing self-determination from self-governance and self-authorization enables us to give due weight to the social and political preconditions for autonomy and underscore that securing these conditions is a matter of social justice. But it also accounts for our important intuitions about autonomy—namely, that a person may be self-governing and self-authorizing to some degree even in situations of crushing oppression where these conditions are severely curtailed, and conversely that a person may enjoy all the freedoms and opportunities necessary for self-determination but nevertheless fail to be self-governing or have a sense of herself as a self-authorizing agent" (2014, 40). The value of distinguishing distinct dimensions of autonomy lies in its ability to accommodate conflicting intuitions where that conflict is not due to fuzzy thought but to the fact that autonomy involves multiple elements and conditions that, frequently, track different and incomparable aspects of human life.

Given these advantages, I have adopted Mackenzie's account of autonomy as a multidimensional concept as a structuring mechanism of this book. Adopting this framework, however, does not entail also adopting Mackenzie's or any particular substantive account of any of the three dimensions. It is, instead, to employ her "conceptual map" which "is an outline of the terrain" (2014, 16). As Mackenzie explains, "the aim of this taxonomy is to map out the different dimensions or axes of the concept of autonomy in a way that makes sense of our complex, and sometimes conflicting, intuitions about autonomy and our diverse autonomy-related social practices" (19). Adopting this conceptual map does imply a substantive commitment to the claim that the concept of autonomy does different work and tracks different things in different contexts. This conceptual map, however, "doesn't resolve debates about how best to understand the different conditions I have identified as relevant to each axis" (19). Theorists who adopt this map may, nevertheless, differ greatly on the question of what the conditions for self-determination, self-governance, or self-authorization are. Theorists may also differ greatly in their views about how the three axes are related to each other. My aim in this book is both to propose new substantive content in relation to each axis as well as to make several contributions to articulating the ways in which these axes are interrelated. Two of the main, overarching claims I defend throughout the book are, first, that the relevance of the constitutively relational to autonomy is not confined to the self-determination axis and, second, that there are important constitutive, and not just causal, relations between the three axes. Both of these claims make clear, and provide a language for articulating, constraints on autonomy that do not rely on a connection between the internalization of oppressive norms and the diminishment of autonomy.

In chapter 1, I consider the self-determination axis of autonomy. As Mackenzie explains, "[s]elf-determination involves having the freedom and opportunities to make and enact choices of practical import to one's life, that is, choices about what to value, who to be, and what to do" (2014, 17). This axis is focused on delineating social conditions that enable or constrain practical control over one's life. It is this axis where constitutively relational elements of autonomy have been developed and where the focus is on external constituting relations rather than on the internal psychological life of the agent whose autonomy is under consideration. The central point of this chapter is to defend the claim that causally relational accounts of the autonomy-inhibiting effects of oppression are insufficient and that a constitutively relational criterion is also required.

I argue that despite their specific theoretical differences, causally relational views share in common what I call "the damage model" of the relevance of oppressive social circumstances to autonomy and that the scope of the damage model is too narrow. I center for analysis examples that bring into focus the ways in which some agents are positioned as preemptively criminal, harassable, and/or expendable because of who others in their social context are encouraged or permitted to be. I propose that members of marginalized groups find their global autonomy constrained when members of dominantly situated groups are encouraged or permitted to have traits that conflict with the assumption that members of marginalized groups have a practical right to self-determination. This criterion not only captures the conjunction of undamaged yet also not fully autonomous, but also shifts attention away from the inner lives of members of marginalized groups and to the problematic, autonomy-inhibiting traits of members of superordinate groups.

Chapters 2–4 focus on self-governance. Self-governance "involves having the skills and capacities necessary to make choices and enact decisions that express, or cohere with, one's reflectively constituted diachronic practical identity" (Mackenzie 2014, 17). Discussions of this axis of autonomy examine the internal psychological lives of agents as they form their identities and values and govern themselves in accordance with those values. Discussions of self-governance typically delineate both competence and authenticity conditions. My aim in chapters 2–4 is to articulate the constitutively relational relevance of the social to considerations of the competence and authenticity conditions of self-governance. One of the common assumptions in the literature is that causally relational accounts of the effects of the external world on an agent are sufficient for capturing the ways in which oppression can diminish self-governance. In chapters 2–4, I trouble this assumption by identifying multiple ways in which the constitutively relational is crucial to understanding how oppressive social circumstances can diminish the self-governance of marginalized agents.

Chapter 2 examines one aspect of the competence condition. Competence conditions specify the requirements for engaging in self-constructive and self-expressive activities. My focus in chapter 2 is on competence with respect to self-expressive activities. I argue that while competence has been taken as an individualistic feature of agents, some competencies central to self-expressive activities should be rendered communally. While all of us sometimes find ourselves in social circumstances where we are thwarted in our desired activities and choices, members of marginally situated groups face pervasive and systemic interpersonal barriers to realizing the ordinary sorts of desires that members of dominantly situated groups do not encounter. My central claim in this chapter is that a constitutively relational, communal competence condition needs to be added to the standard, individual competence condition in order to capture the relevance to self-governance of situations involving the conjunction of relational properties and systemic injustice. The proposed communal competence condition provides a mechanism for articulating the ways in which an unjust lack of participation from others can inappropriately truncate the scope of an agent's self-expressive activities. One place where the communal competence condition is especially important is in considerations of the relationship between autonomy and epistemic injustice. I examine how social contexts marked by epistemic injustice can frustrate the desires of members of marginalized groups by withholding the communal resources required to achieve ordinary relational properties, properties like being believed and being understood. I argue that in contexts of epistemic injustice members of marginalized groups are constrained in the scope of what they can intend to achieve in particular social domains and that my proposed communal competence condition provides a language for articulating the constraint on autonomy these agents face.

Chapter 3 focuses on the competencies needed for self-constructive activities. In addition to the competencies needed for self-expressive activities, competencies are also needed for self-constructive activities. Central to being a self-governing agent is the ability to define and redefine one's practical identity in response to new experiences. In this chapter, I examine the relationship between socially available hermeneutical resources and the self-creative aspect of self-governance. I anchor my analysis in a reading of Édouard Louis's autobiographical novel, *History of Violence*, which provides a rich account of an agent (the main character Édouard) attempting to gain self-understanding and revise his identity in a situation where he is without adequate hermeneutical resources. I articulate three points of connection between autonomy and the availability of adequate hermeneutical resources. First, I consider how the self-creative aspect of self-governance can be stymied when the available hermeneutical resources are inadequate for interpreting one's experiences. I argue that adequate hermeneutical resources are important not only for an agent's continued motivation toward self-understanding and self-definition but also because they provide the materials out of which self-understanding and self-definition are constituted. Second, I examine Édouard's response to the unavailability of the hermeneutical resources needed to make sense of his experiences and argue that his response expresses a communicative need. This communicative need centers the social dimensions of self-understanding and self-definition in situations of hermeneutical inadequacy. Finally, I draw on some of Édouard's attempts to fulfill this communicative need in order to articulate two ways in which communicative exchanges fail and thus fail to meet the needs of agents who are attempting to deepen the available hermeneutical resources through communication with others. In particular, I suggest that attempts to deepen the hermeneutical resources needed for self-understanding and self-definition flounder in contexts where one's words are instrumentalized for extraneous purposes or where one's communicative attempts are mired in sets of historical misunderstandings of one's identity.

Chapter 4 focuses on self-governance and authenticity. In addition to competence conditions, which are the focus of chapters 2 and 3, many accounts of self-governance also include some form of an authenticity condition. Authenticity conditions are meant to provide a mechanism for determining which features of the self, which values, traits, and desires, fall within the scope of successful self-governance.

Standard accounts of the authenticity condition focus on an agent's assessment of a trait, on whether she maintains the relevant sort of pro-attitude toward her characteristics and motivations. While theorists differ about what the necessary pro-attitude is (identification, endorsement, nonalienation), the presence or absence of the relevant pro-attitude determines whether or not a particular characteristic is authentic. Authentic characteristics are thought to issue from or be in line with an agent's true self, while inauthentic ones are considered in some way "foreign" to that self. One of the main tasks of the authenticity condition is to address how unwanted features of the self can diminish self-governance insofar as these features and the desires and actions motivated by these features do not fall within the scope of an agent's value system. Typical examples in the literature include what one does while in the grip of an unwanted drug addiction or under duress or subject to coercion.

In chapter 4, I consider the relevance to autonomy of unwanted characteristics that have a particular constitutively relational structure, a structure that combines (a) something the agent deeply values with (b) unjust sociopolitical conditions to jointly constitute (c) an unwanted feature of the self. I center for analysis two examples of constitutively relational emotions (loneliness and bitterness) that are structured by politically supported or imposed forms of failed relationality. I argue that the authenticity condition is not a useful way to discuss unwanted aspects of the self that are not simply influenced by others and our pasts but are constituted by the unjust relations in which we stand. Instead, I argue that loneliness and bitterness, two constitutively relational characteristics that are constituted in part by something an agent deeply values and in part by a failure of desired relationality, provide examples for analysis that allow a focus on the interplay between one's values and one's social context. The diminishment of autonomy that arises from this interplay is best understood as arising from the way that constraints on self-determination also affect self-governance. While constraints on self-determination can affect the inner life of an agent *causally*, by decreasing motivation to act on one's values or when agents internalize the problematic norms reflected in the constraints they face, constraints on self-determination can also partially *constitute* elements of an agent's motivational system without getting purchase through the agent's sense of motivation or values.

Chapter 5 focuses on the self-authorization axis of autonomy. Mackenzie explains that self-authorization "involves regarding oneself as having the *normative authority* to be self-determining and self-governing. In other words, it involves regarding oneself as authorized to exercise practical control over one's life, to determine one's own reasons for action, and to define one's values and identity-shaping commitments" (2014, 18). An agent's ability to take ownership for herself by occupying the relevant position of authority is typically thought to depend on the presence of appropriate forms of social recognition. In chapter 5, I focus on two main questions about the relationship between self-authorization and social recognition. The first concerns the perspective of the agent: what are the conditions under which she, from her subject position, is willing and able to answer for herself? I argue that a causal rather than a constitutively relational account of the importance of social recognition is both empirically more plausible and politically important. While one of my main aims in the book is to center the insights afforded by considering the constitutively relational aspects of autonomy, in this case I argue that the constitutively relational account has the undesirable consequence of problematically truncating the scope of the claims marginalized agents can autonomously make. The causal account I defend leaves room for agents to be in a position rightfully to claim authority as answerable for themselves even from within contexts where they fail to receive appropriate social recognition. This brings into focus a second perspective on the relationship between social recognition and answerability. Specifically, social mal- and misrecognition may not damage an agent's motivation or ability to answer for herself, but they may practically de-authorize agents from occupying their rightful position as answerable. I examine how some subtle forms of social mal- and misrecognition displace an agent's first-personal, experiential perspective from the sphere of answerability and replace it with a projected, third-personal perspective. Since it is an agent's first-personal experiential perspective that grounds her authority as answerable for herself, I argue that these practices preclude an agent from actively occupying a position of authority and thus constrain her right to answer for herself. While I argue against a constitutively relational account of the relation between social recognition and answerability when considering the question from the perspective of the subjectivity of the agent, I argue for a constitutively relational account of what it means actively to occupy a position of authority as answerable for oneself.

14 INTRODUCTION

Each chapter centers for analysis social conditions and examples that are distinct from the kinds of conditions and examples that motivate concerns about socialization, the internalization of oppressive norms, and the diminishment of autonomy. While the insights generated by concerns about socialization and internalized oppression are valuable, I aim to show that they are insufficient for capturing the interplay between oppressive social conditions and autonomy. Centering a different set of examples, in my view, provides material that points to the importance of the constitutively relational in articulating the constraints on autonomy members of marginalized communities face. My central aim in the book is to show both how the constitutively relational matters to each axis of autonomy and to articulate constitutively relational, and not just causal, connections between the different axes of autonomy.

1

Living with Who Others Get to Be

Self-Determination and Status

1.1. Introduction

Personal autonomy theorists seek to articulate the conditions under which one's life, decisions, actions, and values can meaningfully be said to be one's own.[1] The *ownness* of one's life, globally speaking, and of one's decisions, actions, and values, however, is not indexed to the level of detachment one achieves from one's history, relationships, and sociopolitical context. Contemporary theorists recognize that we are thoroughly socialized and social beings who are in many ways dependent upon and depended upon by others. Contemporary theorists, that is, take seriously the intricate ways in which we are socially embedded.

Many theorists recognize not only that we are socially embedded but also that the sociopolitical spheres in which we find ourselves are marked by subtle and not so subtle forms of inequality and oppression. The social realities of having a racialized identity in a racist context and/or of being a woman in a sexist context and/or of being queer in a heteronormative context, to give just a few examples, are rightly assumed relevant to considerations of personal autonomy. In what ways and to what extent being a member of a partially subordinated social identity is relevant to personal autonomy, however, is contentious.[2]

Attempts to account for the significance of oppression for personal autonomy can be divided, very broadly, into causally relational and constitutively relational explanations. On causally relational treatments of autonomy, the question of whether X's choices, decisions, motivations, and life are

---

[1] This chapter is a moderately revised version of my article "Personal Autonomy, Social Identity, and Oppressive Social Contexts," originally published in 2017 in *Hypatia* 32(2): 312–328.
[2] I use the phrase "partially subordinated social identity" in order to capture the point that relations of oppression and inequality partially structure but do not exhaust the meanings of these social identities.

autonomous can be answered by examining the internal life of X. The external world, on these views, affects autonomy insofar as it has a causal effect on the agent's psychology. For example, loving and supportive familial relations may cause an agent to develop a strong sense of self-worth which contributes to her ability to form her own values. Oppressive social norms, on the other hand, may be internalized and cause an agent to value some of the features of her own oppression in a way that is detrimental to her autonomy. Constitutively relational treatments of autonomy, however, take the external world to be more directly relevant to autonomy. The relations in which we stand in the external world are, in some instances, constitutive features of what it means to be autonomous. For example, being incarcerated may constitute a constraint on autonomy independently of the psychological response of the person who is incarcerated.[3]

My interest here is in examining the senses in which membership in such partially subordinated social identities, identities that mark one for various forms of oppressive treatment, affect one's autonomy. I argue that causally relational explanations are insufficient for identifying the autonomy-inhibiting aspects of being a member of a partially subordinated social identity and articulate one required constitutively relational criterion.[4] Ultimately, I argue that one's global autonomy is narrowed when one is attributed a status incompatible with the assumption that one enjoys the freedom conditions necessary for autonomy. The constitutively relational condition I propose is meant to articulate the sense in which aspects of some social identities constrain the autonomy of members of other social identities. I argue, more specifically, that the implicit social permissibility of subjecting members of socially subordinated identities to violent, or at least violating, forms of interference is incompatible with unconstrained global self-determination.

---

[3] While *explanations* of the relations between oppression and autonomy can be divided into causally relational and constitutively relational accounts, nothing prevents hybrid *theories* that combine both sorts of explanations. Those who elaborate the constitutively relational connections between autonomy and oppression typically also include detailed analysis of the relevant causally relational factors (Mackenzie 2014; Oshana 2006). Those more focused on the significance of causally relational explanations sometimes also include, or at least make space for, constitutively relational elements. Friedman, for example claims that "[t]o be autonomous, someone should have a significant array of opportunities to act in ways that reflect what deeply matters to her" (2003, 18). Nevertheless, even in hybrid views, causally relational and constitutively relational explanations are distinct kinds of explanations. My point in focusing on these different kinds of explanations is (a) to draw attention to the commonalities that hold across different kinds of causally relational explanations, (b) to articulate both the value and the limitations of causally relational explanations, and (c) to articulate the additional kind of explanatory power constitutively relational explanations can offer.

[4] In subsequent chapters, I develop and defend additional constitutively relational conditions.

I begin, in section 1.2, by articulating the general problem and the important motivating dilemma that causally relational explanations are focused on addressing and suggest that despite significant differences among the various types of causally relational accounts, these accounts share what I call "the damage model" of the relevance to autonomy of membership in partially subordinated social identities. On the damage model, sexist, racist, and heterosexist social environments affect one's autonomy by causing certain sorts of damage to members of partially subordinated social identities.

In section 1.3, I introduce a different sort of example for analysis, an example that generates a dilemma distinct from the one driving the debate among different sorts of causally relational explanations. Briefly, recent literature on the theme of personal autonomy and oppression has been focused largely on resolving a particular dilemma about autonomy and women's agency: how are we to assess the autonomy of women who are motivated by values, have desires, and make decisions that coincide with particular features of sexist oppression? Although analyses directed at resolving this dilemma allow us to trace an important way in which oppressive social circumstances may affect autonomy, they do not exhaust the concerns for autonomy generated by subordinating social environments. I introduce examples that have to do not primarily with what an agent values or desires but with problematic attributions of status that attach to one qua membership in certain social identities. In particular, I will focus on analyzing the significance to autonomy of living among others who are permitted, explicitly or implicitly, to be harassers, to engage in racial profiling, and to treat members of some oppressed social groups as expendable. I argue that a constitutively relational criterion is needed in order to identify the ways in which who some get to *be* constitute constraints on the autonomy of others.

In section 1.4, I articulate a positive argument for the claim that we should want to employ a constitutively relational condition, and in section 1.5 I draw on, but ultimately depart from, Marina Oshana's constitutively relational account of autonomy in order to articulate a minimal constitutively relational autonomy-securing criterion.

1.2. Social Subordination and the Damage Model

Most discussions of the ways in which a person's autonomy is made vulnerable by membership in a partially subordinated social identity focus on delineating causal explanations of the relationship between autonomy and oppression as part of an attempt to solve the socialization problem.[5] Contemporary autonomy theorists start from an acknowledgment that personal autonomy is not a matter of excavating or discovering a presocial self, untainted by socialization; we are all thoroughly socialized beings. Socialization per se, therefore, is not necessarily a threat to personal autonomy and in many ways enables one by providing the relationships, skills, and capacities necessary for autonomy. Socialization, however, even if understood as in some ways coercive, is not all the same. As Diana Tietjens Meyers explains, "The question is not whether to have a coercive or a noncoercive form of childhood socialization. Since there is no such thing as noncoercive childhood socialization, but since socialization is an inescapable feature of civilization, some form of coercive socialization must be justifiable. Indeed, it is not the coerciveness of socialization that generally draws fire. It is when socialization harms people that the process itself falls under suspicion" (1989, 207). Resolving the socialization problem, therefore, involves delineating the criteria by which we can distinguish benign or enabling socialization from harmful, autonomy-inhibiting socialization.

The socialization problem has been especially vexing for feminists and has been complicated by the following dilemma. On the one hand, it has long been acknowledged that sexism works, in part, by conditioning women to desire and value the mechanisms of our own subordination; this acknowledgment raises suspicions about whether desires, preferences, and motivating values are autonomous when they coincide with or overlap with the set of desires, preferences, and motivating values that have typically been thought to perpetuate sexist inequality. On the other hand, feminists are also rightly wary of denying agency and a voice to women who claim that their desires and values are autonomous.

In response to this sort of dilemma, theorists attempt to articulate the conditions that some action, desire, motivating value, and so on must meet in order to count as autonomous. Most responses to this dilemma are causally relational accounts which can be broadly divided into strongly substantivist,[6] weakly substantivist, and proceduralist explanations. Causally relational versions of strongly substantivist positions evaluate as

---

[5] As noted above, many theories are hybrid theories; nevertheless most extended analyses focus on the significance of causally relational factors. For an extended constitutively relational account of the relations between autonomy and oppression, see Oshana (2006). I engage Oshana's work in later sections of this chapter.

[6] Not all strongly substantivist positions are causally relational positions, but some causally relational positions are strongly substantivist. Those that require agents' values and desires to have a

necessarily nonautonomous certain values and desires because of their content, whereas proceduralist views are content-neutral; any desire or value can be autonomous provided it passes an autonomy-securing procedure. Weakly substantivist views, though not judging values and desires nonautonomous because of their content, hold that something more than a procedure is needed to decide the case, and this something more is something that must be true of the subject whose values and desires are being evaluated. For example, a strongly substantive view might reject a desire for subordination to another as necessarily nonautonomous because of the content of that desire. A proceduralist view would evaluate the autonomy of this desire according to whether it passes an autonomy-securing procedure. A weakly substantive view would not necessarily take this desire to be nonautonomous on the grounds of its content but would require something more of the agent than completing the relevant procedure. For example, the presence of appropriate self-evaluative attitudes like self-trust and self-respect would also be required. My point here is not to enter into the debate among proponents of these different sorts of causally relational views; instead I want to draw attention to a commonality that holds across the different views when articulating the ways that living in oppressive circumstances can undermine an agent's autonomy. In trying to understand how social subordination may diminish autonomy, they focus on the ways in which agents can be damaged by internalized oppression.

Natalie Stoljar (2000) and Susan Babbitt (1993), for example, who represent strongly substantivist views, require agents to value certain things (autonomy itself, for example) and prohibit the valuation of other things (subordination, for example). Failures to value or to repudiate the right sorts of things are, for Stoljar and Babbitt, explicable in terms of the damage done to agents through oppressive socialization. Stoljar articulates the feminist intuition that "preferences influenced by oppressive norms of femininity cannot be autonomous" (2000, 95). The reason they cannot be autonomous is because of their content (109). Subjects who have such preferences, Stoljar argues, are unable to see that they have internalized false norms. Their capacity to see these norms as false is what is lacking or damaged, on Stoljar's account (109). For Babbitt, autonomy requires that one satisfy one's objective interest in flourishing, but "[i]n situations involving ideological oppression,

---

certain content are causally relational, whereas those whose substantive content lies in specifying acceptable social relations are constitutively relational.

an individual may fail to possess preferences and desires that adequately reflect an interest in her own human flourishing because she has been beaten down by the circumstances of her situation" (1993, 246). Oppression, for Babbitt, can damage agents in ways that undermine their ability to value their own flourishing. "The effects of oppression" Babbitt explains, "may be such that people are psychologically damaged, possessing interests and desires that reflect their subservient social status" (246).

Most theorists, however, concede that desires, values, and actions, even when connected to gender stereotypes, expectations, and forms of oppression, have a more complex relation to autonomy than can be revealed exclusively by examining their content.[7] These theories, however, share with strongly substantivist views a model in which oppressive circumstances are relevant to autonomy because of the damage they cause agents. Specifically, agents can be damaged in the self-reflexive attitudes required for autonomy, in the dispositions required for autonomy, and/or in the competencies required for autonomy.

Many theorists identify the possession of certain self-referential attitudes as necessary for autonomy. Sonya Charles (2010), for example, identifies damage to self-worth, which makes a woman complicit in her own subordination, as the factor that is most important for considerations of whether or not some decision is autonomous. Catriona Mackenzie, as well as Joel Anderson and Axel Honneth, hold that oppressive socialization undermines one's autonomy competency by undermining the necessary self-reflexive attitudes of self-respect, self-trust, and self-esteem (Anderson and Honneth 2005, 127–49; Mackenzie 2000, 124–50).[8]

Paul Benson, in his weakly substantivist view, follows a similar trajectory; for Benson "autonomy's normative substance resides in agents' attitudes toward their own authority to speak and answer for their decisions" (2005a, 25).[9] Agents' attitudes toward this authority depend on having self-referential attitudes of self-worth and self-confidence. Benson explains that internalized oppression may affect one's self-worth and self-confidence in a way that undermines an agent's ability to maintain the relevant sort of authority. He asks us, for example, to consider "someone who, on the basis of race, has

---

[7] For further discussion see Meyers (2014) and Santiago (2005).

[8] Anderson and Honneth (2005), while identifying self-trust, self-respect, and self-esteem, do not think that these are merely personal traits; they are constituted in part by an agent's psychology and in part by one's social position. I return to this point in chapter 5.

[9] For Benson's earlier views of the significance of oppression to autonomy, views that also articulate the problem in terms of the damage internalized oppression causes, see Benson (1991, 1994, 2000).

systematically been treated as socially invisible, as lacking the dignity of a person and eligibility to participate in distinctly personal forms of relationship, such as friendship, or familial love" (2005b, 111). On Benson's view, if agents in such a position internalize their social invisibility, this can "defeat agents' capacities to take ownership of what they do" (112). Oppression, therefore, on Benson's view, impedes autonomy when it "defeats" the capacities agents need to take ownership of their actions.[10]

Proceduralist views, such as those developed by Meyers (2002) and Christman (2009), also consider the damage done by oppression. On Meyers's agential-competence view, autonomy depends on the development and exercise of a set of autonomy competencies. For Meyers, "autonomous people have well-developed, well-coordinated repertoires of agentic skills and can call on them routinely as they reflect on themselves and their lives and as they reach decisions about how best to go on" (2002, 19).[11] Oppressive circumstances can interfere with both the development and the exercise of

---

[10] Westlund holds a similar view about the importance of answerability; the difference between a woman who autonomously chooses a particular subordinate position and one who is nonautonomous in her choice depends, in part, on whether she has a disposition to hold herself answerable to others. Westlund explains that "autonomy in choice and action . . . relies (at least in part) on the disposition to hold oneself answerable to external critical perspectives on one's action-guiding commitments" (2009, 28). Westlund does not specifically identify the ways in which living in oppressive circumstances may damage agents' autonomy, but she does hold that "[r]elations of care are causal contributors to the developed capacity for autonomy" (36). It is plausible, therefore, to suppose that Westlund would accept that oppressive circumstances that deprive agents of sufficient care could impede the development of the disposition to hold themselves answerable in ways necessary for autonomous choice and action. Westlund's view, while remaining content-neutral, also incorporates a constitutively relational element. The disposition to hold oneself answerable "requires an irreducibly dialogical form of reflectiveness and responsiveness to others. But this type of relationality, while constitutive, is formal rather than substantive in nature and carries with it no specific value commitments (28).

[11] The specific skills Meyers identifies are "1. Introspection skills that sensitize individuals to their own feelings and desires, that enable them to interpret their subjective experience, and that help them judge how good a likeness a self-portrait is; 2. Communication skills that enable individuals to get the benefit of others' perceptions, background knowledge, insights, advice, and support; 3. Memory skills that enable individuals to recall relevant experiences—not only from their own lives, but also those that associates have recounted or that they have encountered in literature or other art forms; 4. Imagination skills that enable individuals to envisage feasible options—to audition a range of self-images they might adopt and to preview a variety of plot lines their lives might follow; 5. Analytical skills and reasoning skills that enable individuals to assess the relative merits of different visions of what they could be like and precis for future episodes in their life stories; 6. Self-nurturing skills that enable individuals to secure their physical and psychological equilibrium despite missteps and setbacks—that enable them to appreciate the overall worthiness of their self-portraits and their self-narratives, assure themselves of their capacity to carry on when they find their self-portraits wanting or their self-narratives misguided, and sustain their self-respect if they need to correct their self-portraits or revise their self-narratives; 7. Volitional skills that enable individuals to resist pressure to capitulate to convention and enable them to maintain their commitment to the self-portrait and to the continuations of their autobiographies that they consider genuinely their own; 8. Interpersonal skills that enable individuals to join forces to challenge and change cultural regimes and institutional arrangements" (2002, 19; see also Meyers 1989, 76–91).

these skills. As Meyers explains, "this view of autonomy acknowledges the institutionalization of male dominance and the gravity of internalized oppression, both of which impede women's ability to develop and exercise these skills" (21). Oppressive circumstances, therefore, are relevant to autonomy insofar as they damage agents by impeding the development and exercise of these skills.

Christman's proceduralist account also reflects the damage model. Christman claims that the test for whether autonomy obtains with respect to a particular characteristic C depends on both competency requirements and authenticity requirements. With respect to the basic requirements of competence, Christman specifies the following two conditions:

1. The person is competent to effectively form intentions to act on the basis of C. That is, she enjoys the array of competences that are required for her to negotiate socially, bodily, affectively, and cognitively in ways necessary to form effective intentions of the basis of C;
2. The person has the general capacity to critically reflect on C and other basic motivating elements of her psychic and bodily make-up. (2009, 155)

As with the other causally relational views, the autonomy of C could be affected by oppressive social environments if those environments undermine an agent's ability to meet either of these two conditions.

With respect to authenticity, Christman specifies a nonalienation condition. Specifically, C is autonomous if it meets the following conditions:

3. Were the person to engage in sustained critical reflection on C over a variety of conditions in light of the historical processes (adequately described) that gave rise to C; and
4. She would not be alienated from C in the sense of feeling and judging that C cannot be sustained as part of an acceptable autobiographical narrative organized by her diachronic practical identity; and
5. The reflection being imagined is not constrained by reflection-distorting factors. (2009, 155)

A further way, then, in which being a member of a partially subordinated social identity may affect autonomy on Christman's view concerns the concept of alienation. An agent may meet conditions (1), (2), (3), and (5), yet be alienated from the characteristic in question. She may, if she were to engage in the specified type of reflection, realize that she came to have this trait due to the internalization of oppressive norms, and this realization may (although it also may not) cause her to be alienated from the trait.

The predominant model, therefore, for dealing with the ways in which membership in partially subordinated social identities is relevant to autonomy on causally relational accounts is a *damage model*: a model that identifies the damage done to agents as a result of internalized oppression. Oppression may damage or impede the development of the self-reflective attitudes, skills, capacities, and dispositions that are necessary for autonomy and thereby have a negative effect on an oppressed subject's autonomy.

1.3. Beyond the Damage Model

Because theorists are primarily engaged with the task of distinguishing benign or enabling socialization from oppressive socialization, the examples employed in the literature tend to be those that have the following structure: (a) person X thinks she is autonomous with respect to Y, but (b) there are reasons to suspect that X is not autonomous with respect to Y, because (c) Y is somehow problematically connected to the internalization of oppressive norms.[12] Or, to cast the point from the other side of the dilemma: (a) some Z thinks that X is not autonomous with respect to Y (b) because Y is coincidental with some serious aspect of gender oppression, but (c) Z is wrong in her assessment. Common examples of Y include decisions and life plans that reflect oppressive gendered norms: norms such as the expectation that women will be subservient or submissive, that women's worth or value is determined by physical appearance, or that women ought not to claim sexual agency. The animating worry in these examples concerns the coincidence of women's plans, decisions, and values, with gender norms that perpetuate women's subordination.

Causally relational views deal in nuanced ways with the fact that living in oppressive circumstances can, but need not always, damage agents in ways relevant to their autonomy. The criteria offered on the various theories provide essential tools for articulating why one woman who values and is

---

[12] Theorists differ about which exact examples we can put under (b) and about the nature of the connection specified in (c).

motivated by a certain subordinating value may be autonomous while another may not.[13] The values of the former, for example, will pass the relevant procedural tests, and the agent herself will have the relevant set of self-referential attitudes and skills.

Although I think that these theorists are right to consider the causal interplay between oppressive socialization and the inner life of agents when considering the primary motivating dilemma concerning choices that coincide with oppressive norms, identifying the ways that autonomy is affected by oppression nevertheless requires the articulation of a constitutively relational criterion. To illustrate where the need falls, I want to consider an example that has a different structure from those that drive the sorts of dilemmas considered so far.

In explicating her constitutively relational position, Oshana offers an example that is fruitful to elaborate and engage further. Oshana argues for a constitutively relational position, a position that takes the external requirements for autonomy to be the presence of appropriate social relations. The appropriate social relations that autonomous persons enjoy are those that "enable them to direct their lives with a minimum of interference" (2006, 88). Oshana argues that "[i]nterferences threaten autonomy when they relegate persons to a position whereby, in order to live in a self-managed, self-directed fashion, persons must resist the interference, or at least resist the temptation to regard the interference as normal and legitimate, even as they adapt to its presence" (88).

To illustrate this problematic kind of interference, Oshana asks us to consider the adaptation and vigilance "found in response to the phenomenon of racial profiling known as 'Driving While Black.' Statistically, African-American men (and darker complexioned men, more generally) are subject to arbitrary stop-and-searches by law enforcement officials to a disproportionate extent, frequently while driving to work" (2006, 88). Oshana explains, "[T]he issue is that these persons are socially positioned such that they *must*

---

[13] Causally relational strongly substantive views, like those defended by Babbit (1993) and Stoljar (2000), however, are less flexible insofar as the content of certain values precludes autonomy. On these types of views, differences in the autonomy of two agents living in similarly oppressive contexts would be accounted for in terms of whether the agent was damaged by social messages in a way that led to the adoption of a particular prohibited value. For example, persistent messages that one is unworthy of pursuing one's own flourishing may cause an agent to adopt values that conflict with valuing one's own flourishing. For another agent, however, these messages may not damage her in a way that leads to the adoption of problematic values.

adapt to being a person subject to racial profiling, by resistance, or by cunning, or by ingratiation" (90).

I will return in the final section of this chapter to the significance of the claim that agents *must* adapt, but I want, for now, to consider how we should articulate *to what* one is adapting. Persons who are subject to racial profiling must adapt to the fact that they are socially positioned such that they have a certain status: the status of being preemptively assumed criminal. Such a person has this status precisely because other persons, in this case law-enforcement officials, are permitted and/or encouraged to have the trait of being racial profilers.

Members of partially subordinated social identities often live in contexts where they have to occupy a status as a result of who other people, in virtue of their social identities, are permitted to be. For example, Black men and trans women of color live in a social context where they are socially positioned such that they have the status of being expendable. The unconscionable rates of both incarceration and murder that members of these social identities face reveal the presence of this status. Members of these social identities have this status precisely because other persons are permitted and/or encouraged to have traits that position these subjects as expendable. Law-enforcement officials are permitted to engage in racial profiling, and cis-gender men, for example, are permitted violently to enforce a naturalized gender binary. Women and queer subjects, to give another example, live in a social context where they are socially positioned such that they have the status of being harassable. Members of these social identities have this status precisely because other persons are permitted and/or encouraged to be harassers.

A constitutively relational criterion is needed in order fully to articulate how being positioned as preemptively criminal, expendable, and harassable because of who members of other, superordinate identities get to be constrains one's autonomy. Specifically, a constitutively relational criterion is required in order to capture how this positioning in terms of status *itself*, and not just *that* one must react or *how* one reacts to this positioning, matters to autonomy. Causally relational explanations, though they can account for the ways in which such social positioning may damage agents in ways relevant to their autonomy, are not well-adapted to articulating the particular constraint on autonomy generated by these questions of status.

Causally relational theories provide important tools that enable us to claim that an agent's autonomy is compromised when she is alienated from the traits she develops in response to her social position or when one or more of her self-regarding attitudes or autonomy competencies are damaged by the internalization of oppressive norms. The tools provided by causally relational views, however, are not suited to capturing the ways in which someone's autonomy is narrowed by the fact that others are allowed to have traits that position her as harassable, expendable, and criminal, in cases where she is neither alienated from her response to these facts nor damaged in ways that affect her self-regarding attitudes or autonomy competencies.[14]

For example, suppose a subject is deeply embedded in caring and resistant communities such that she enjoys the kinds of support that enable her to develop the necessary self-reflexive attitudes, dispositions, skills, and competencies. This person is fortunate enough to enjoy the kinds of community that can stop one from internalizing messages about one's expendability, harassability, or presumed criminality such that her self-regarding attitudes and autonomy competencies are undamaged by the oppressive context.

Moreover, suppose that a general governing value in this person's life is a commitment to being able to read her social situation and respond practically and with a range of affect to the reality of the various contexts in which she finds herself. In all spheres of her life, she is committed to taking appropriate action in response to what she understands of the world around her, and she is committed to maintaining a complex emotional life that does not ignore the circumstances in which she finds herself. Under the rubric of this governing value, she reacts to the fact that others are permitted and/or encouraged to be harassers by (a) engaging with others in social protests, education projects, and an assortment of resistant practices aimed at changing this feature of her social world and by cultivating a healthy sense of outrage about this aspect of her social position, and (b) she employs a number of different strategies in her daily life depending on the context and what she's doing at the time. Sometimes she avoids situations where she suspects she will be harassed (she crosses the road rather than walk past a raucous and intoxicated group of men), sometimes she aggressively confronts those engaged in harassing behavior either of her or of other people, and sometimes, in the face of harassment, she tries as quickly as possible to forget it so she can return to daydreaming or planning her day. Suppose, also, that her governing value and the particular ways she instantiates this value in her daily

---

[14] My point here is not to criticize the tools developed by causally relational accounts; these tools were developed to deal with specific problems and they do so in valuable ways. Rather, my point is to suggest that additional conceptual apparatus is needed to capture the ways in which oppression can diminish autonomy even if it does not damage an agent's psychology.

life pass the relevant proceduralist test; she is satisfied with how she is governing her life.

On causally relational accounts, this person is autonomous. Since she has managed to escape the potentially *damaging* effects of having a social identity that positions her as harassable, and her governing values and the way she instantiates them pass the relevant procedures, there is nothing more to say about the ways her social context affects her autonomy.

There is, however, something more to say about cases like this. Specifically, what causally relational views miss about the ways oppression can narrow autonomy is the aspect of oppression that is constraining rather than damaging. In the next section, I support the claim that we should want to say that an agent's autonomy is narrowed even in cases like this, but first let me briefly clarify what I'm not claiming. First, I am not claiming that causally relational theorists are wrong to claim that this agent's values, desires, and actions are autonomous. In order to articulate the sense in which her autonomy is constrained, we will need to look at her autonomy as a person rather than at the autonomy of particular desires, values, and actions. Second, I am not claiming, simply, that she is nonautonomous because her strategies of prudential rationality are adaptations to oppressive features of her social environment. My critique is not, that is, best cast in terms of the debate about whether adaptive preferences can be autonomous.[15] I would agree with those who judge this agent's adaptive preferences to be autonomous. What I am claiming is that even if she is autonomous with respect to her motivating values, her choices, and so on, there is still some significant sense in which *she* is not fully autonomous. There is a sense in which certain aspects of the ways it is permissible to treat her in the world put a constraint on the extent to which we can say that her life is her own.

1.4. An Alternative Dilemma

Many who advance causally relational accounts rightly worry about placing constitutively relational constraints on autonomy because such constraints may obscure the agency of those who are marginalized.[16] I, however, want

---

[15] For discussions of autonomy and adaptive preferences, see Khader (2011, 2012); Christman (2014a); Stoljar (2014); Mackenzie (2015).

[16] One particular worry, a worry that is also generated by causally relational versions of strongly substantivist theories, is that including constitutive constraints is perfectionist. Christman argues that strongly substantivist theories, including strongly substantivist views that require agents to stand

to articulate a positive reason for introducing a constitutively relational criterion. The dilemma causally relational accounts of the role of oppression in limiting autonomy seeks to resolve concerns the possibility of a coincidence between adopting oppressive and subordinating values and being autonomous. Taking care to articulate the conditions of this possibility is important so as not preemptively to silence what members of oppressed social identities have to say about their own lives. As outlined above, however, living in oppressive circumstances generates additional kinds of problems for autonomy. In order to capture the nature of these constraints, an alternative kind of causal story is needed.

Causally relational theories can support a particular kind of story about cases where who others get to be, in their social context, undermines autonomy. Specifically, they provide the tools needed for agents to examine their *responses* to who other people in their social context get to be. They can provide a language for articulating the problems in cases where who other people get to be damages agents' autonomy competencies, dispositions, and self-reflexive attitudes or causes agents to be alienated from some characteristic they have developed in response to their social position. What causally relational theories cannot do, however, is provide conceptual space for articulating the conjunction of internally undamaged and not alienated from one's traits yet nevertheless lacking in full autonomy. In my view, however, the fact that some people are permitted and/or encouraged to be harassers, to engage in racial profiling, and to treat some others as expendable narrows the autonomy of those subject to such treatment even when they do not suffer internal damage or alienation from their own responses.

We should preserve conceptual space to articulate a narrowing of autonomy distinct from damage and alienation mainly with a view to the kind

---

in particular sorts of social relations, are perfectionist. Perfectionism, Christman explains, "is the view that values and moral principles can be valid for a person independent of her judgment of those values and principles" (2009, 173). I concede that my view is perfectionist. If an agent were to insist that having a social status where other people are allowed to harass her is something she values, she would, on my view, be nonautonomous just in case other people are in fact allowed to harass her. But two points. Claiming that persons cannot autonomously value being socially positioned such that members of other social groups are randomly and capriciously permitted to harass them or treat them as expendable does not seem, immediately, to raise the same kinds of worries about agency as claiming that a woman cannot autonomously value deference or various sorts of subordinate positions. This suggests to me that some care needs to be taken to distinguish different kinds of unequal social relations. Some forms of unequal social relations will have a complex relation to autonomy, and others, like the ones I discuss here, will not. Second, although an agent would not be autonomous in the unlikely case that she values having a social status where other people are allowed to harass her just in case other people are in fact allowed to harass her, I am not suggesting that her values are necessarily nonautonomous.

of causal story we can tell about how oppression affects autonomy. Causally relational views of the autonomy-impinging effects of the kinds of oppression I am considering necessarily implicate the agent's psychology in the causal story of her diminished autonomy. The causal story of the relevance of oppression for autonomy is one in which oppressive social circumstances cause damage to an agent by impeding the development or the exercise of the skills and capacities needed for autonomy, by damaging the self-referential attitudes needed for autonomy, or by causing her to be alienated from some aspect of who she is. Although external oppressive social circumstances play a role in explaining such an agent's diminished autonomy, these social relations are not the immediate cause of her diminished autonomy. Instead X, the agent, is the immediate cause of her diminished autonomy; it is something about her, about her competencies or her self-referential attitudes, for example, that explains why she is not autonomous. She is, in every instance, implicated in the causal story of her diminished autonomy. What is problematic about this kind of story is that there is no space to claim that it is *only* the agent's social context and not also the agent herself that causally contributes to her diminished autonomy. The causal story of someone's diminished autonomy will often involve an immediate cause in the agent, but we should preserve conceptual space for cases where the immediate and exclusive cause of an agent's narrowed autonomy is explicable in terms of her social context.

1.5. Concluding Thoughts: A Constitutively Relational Condition

In order to capture more fully the ways in which members of subordinated social identities find their autonomy threatened, it is necessary to consider how living in an oppressive social context can constitute agents as constrained rather than damaged. I propose that members of social identity X find their global autonomy constrained when they are positioned in social systems of power such that some aspect of another social identity Y conflicts with the assumption that members of social identity X enjoy a practical right to self-determination. In the specific cases I consider, cases where others are permitted to harass, engage in racial profiling, and treat as expendable, one's autonomy is practically constrained because one is positioned as someone with the status of being appropriately subjected to violent or violating interference; this status, I suggest, is in conflict with a freedom condition necessary for unconstrained global self-determination.

Let me turn to Oshana's account in order to clarify the constitutively relational criterion I wish to articulate. Although Oshana does not undervalue or ignore causally relational effects on an agent's psychology, she claims that "[a]utonomous persons have *de facto* power and authority over the management of their lives within a framework of standards they set for themselves and their autonomy is partly constituted by exogenous phenomena—that is, by relations extrinsic to their psychology" (2006, 87–88). These extrinsic features identify appropriate social relations, where "appropriate" picks out social relations that "enable them to direct their lives with a minimum of interference" (88). Oshana argues that "[i]nterferences threaten autonomy when they relegate persons to a position whereby, in order to live in a self-managed, self-directed fashion, persons must resist the interference, or at least resist the temptation to regard the interference as normal and legitimate, even as they adapt to its presence" (88).

For Oshana, therefore, "[w]hat is at issue in the case of racial profiling and similar states of affairs is not simply the frequency or the predictability of interferences, nor that a person's self-determination is abridged in what some regard as relatively minor ways, nor that only certain persons suffer such abridgements to a disproportionate extent. Rather, the issue is that these persons are socially positioned such that they *must* adapt to being a person subject to racial profiling, by resistance, or by cunning, or by ingratiation" (2006, 90). The problem, from Oshana's perspective, is that in order to live in a self-directed way, a person subject to racial profiling must adapt to an inappropriate sort of interference. On Oshana's view, the issue is one of being problematically constrained with an imperative to do something.

I agree with Oshana's claim that being constrained by an imperative to do something because of one's social position narrows one's autonomy, but I want to suggest that there is an additional problem. This problem is that who some people get to be because of their membership in particular superordinated identities puts a practical constraint on other people's autonomy. Insofar as, for example, men and cis-gender straight people can be harassers of women and trans subjects, women and trans subjects have a social status that constrains their autonomy.

In order to explicate the nature of this constraint, I take up Mackenzie's suggestion that rather than viewing autonomy as a unitary concept, we should understand "that the concept of autonomy involves three distinct but causally interdependent dimensions or axes: self-determination, self-governance, and self-authorization" (2014, 17).[17] It is the distinction between self-determination and self-governance that is useful for articulating the scope and the content of my constitutively relational condition. Mackenzie explains that self-determination "involves having the freedom and opportunities to make and enact choices of practical import to one's life, that is, choices about what to value, who to be, and what to do" (17). Mackenzie explains that satisfying the freedom and opportunity conditions for self-determination will involve identifying the "external, structural conditions for individual autonomy" (17).[18] The second axis, self-governance, "identifies internal conditions for autonomy, specifically competence and authenticity conditions" (18), and "involves having the skills and capacities necessary to make choices and enact decisions that express, or cohere with, one's reflectively constituted diachronic practical identity" (17). The advantage of distinguishing these two axes, as Mackenzie argues, is that one can identify external conditions that must be in place in order for one to be self-determining, without thereby implying that agents who live in contexts where those conditions are not satisfied lack self-governance (23–24). It leaves open, in other words, space to articulate certain kinds of threats to autonomy that come from living in oppressive circumstances without requiring that agents be internally damaged in the competencies, skills, and self-reflective attitudes necessary for autonomy.

The content of the constitutively relational condition I propose is best explicated as one of the freedom conditions required for global self-determination. While particular instances of harassment, for example, undermine one's episodic self-determination, living among those empowered to harass constrains one's global self-determination. Specifically, I suggest that one of the freedom conditions necessary for global self-determination is freedom from living among those whose identities include aspects that systematically and pervasively position one as someone for whom interference is appropriate/tolerated. If members of social identity A are implicitly

---

[17] For further details about Mackenzie's framework, please see the introduction.
[18] Some may object that the self-determination branch in general, and my proposed criterion in particular, are relevant to an agent's freedom but not to her autonomy. I find it problematic to take certain freedoms as unrelated to personal autonomy. Following Oshana, I take a person's life to consist of more than just her psychological profile and thus take the autonomy of a person's life to require more than the autonomy of her psychological profile; it requires also a degree of practical control over her affairs (2006, 49–52). Certain freedoms are necessary for a person to enjoy practical control over her life. Taking an agent's autonomy as a person to be entirely distinct from questions about the freedoms that agent has is problematically reductive about what it means to live autonomously because it reduces the autonomy of a person's life to the autonomy of her psychological profile.

or explicitly permitted to harass, subject to racial profiling, and/or treat as expendable members of social identity B, this means that members of social identity A are empowered to interfere with members of social identity B. If members of social identity A are empowered to interfere with members of social identity B, then members of social identity B are socially positioned vis-à-vis members of social identity A as people for whom interference is appropriate/tolerated. And being socially positioned as someone for whom interference is appropriate/tolerated in a particular context is incompatible with enjoying the practical recognition of someone with the right to be self-determining in that context. In other words, a real and practical right to self-determination is conceptually incompatible with occupying a status that positions one as someone for whom interference is appropriate/tolerated.

Although causally relational theories provide important tools for analyzing many aspects of the significance of oppressive social circumstances for autonomy, they do not adequately capture the problems that arise for autonomy from the traits and behaviors members of superordinated identities are permitted. My constitutively relational criterion will, I hope, provide a direct way to articulate the constraint to autonomy that arises, not from damage, but from socially enabled traits in those who occupy dominant positions.

2
Self-Governance, Self-Expressive Activities, and Communal Competence

2.1. Introduction

Those who enjoy personal autonomy are characterized as self-determining, self-governing, and self-authorizing.[1] In chapter 1, I argued for a constitutively relational element of self-determination. In this chapter, I consider how some of the ordinary, everyday experiences of members of marginalized groups should prompt a reconsideration of self-governance; specifically, I argue for a constitutively relational aspect of self-governance.

Other people, who they get to be and what they do, how they interact with us, their assumptions and ways of being in the world have significant consequences for the quality and texture of our lives. Others can be sources of and participants in, for example, experiences of joy, love, humor, engagement, comfort, care, camaraderie, and struggle. They can also, in both haphazard and systematic ways, frustrate our attempts to live, to be, and to do as we want. While all of us sometimes find ourselves in social circumstances where our true identities and desires remain unrecognized and where we are thwarted in our desired activities and choices, members of marginally situated groups face pervasive and systemic interpersonal barriers to realizing the ordinary sorts of desires that members of dominantly situated groups do not encounter. I argue that the ways in which members of marginalized groups are constrained in the scope of what they can intend to

---

[1] Mackenzie brings clarity to the concept of personal autonomy by suggesting that "autonomy is a multidimensional, rather than a unitary, concept" that consists of "three distinct, but causally interdependent, dimensions or axes of autonomy: self-determination, self-governance, and self-authorization" (2014, 15). "*Self-determination* involves having the freedom and opportunities to make and enact choices of practical import to one's life" (17). "*Self-governance* involves having the skills and capacities necessary to make choices and enact decisions that express, or cohere with, one's reflectively constituted diachronic practical identity" (17), and "*self-authorization* involves regarding oneself as having *normative authority* to be self-determining and self-governing" (18). For further elaboration, please see the introduction.

achieve in particular social domains point to the insufficiency of the individualistic conception of the competence condition for self-governance.

While theorists differ about how to specify these conditions, self-governance involves meeting two types of conditions: authenticity conditions and competence conditions.[2] "Authenticity conditions specify what it means to be self-governing with respect to one's motivational structure, i.e., what it means for a choice, value, commitment, or reason to be one's own" (Mackenzie 2014, 31). Competence conditions specify the range of competences, or skills, a person must possess in order adequately to participate in the creation of the self and the expression of that self in the world.

Recent work on the competence conditions for self-governance has focused primarily on replacing an overly rationalistic conception of these conditions with a model that incorporates a more holistic and realistic conception of the human agent. While there is general agreement that rational and volitional skills are necessary for autonomy competence, these skills do not exhaust the set of skills required for self-governance. Thus relational theorists have expanded this list to include "emotional skills, such as emotional responsiveness, and being able to interpret one's own and others' emotions; imaginative skills, which are necessary for envisaging alternative possible courses of action, or 'imagining oneself otherwise' and engaging in self-transformative activities; and social or dialogical skills required for self-understanding or self-knowledge" (Mackenzie 2014, 33).[3] While these developments concerning the kinds of skills required for competence are important, they share with earlier theories a model of competence that takes one's social relations and social environment as causally but not constitutively relevant to self-governance.

As I argued in chapter 1, causally relational treatments of the connections between autonomy and social context employ a damage model. Social relations diminish autonomy in those cases where they damage an agent's psychology in ways relevant to achieving autonomy. In the case of competence conditions, what is damaged is either an agent's ability to develop or an agent's ability to employ one or more of the skills relevant to meeting the competence condition. Restrictive social environments, for example, may fail to supply the life experiences needed to develop these skills or may undermine an agent's belief that she is worthy of employing these skills.

---

[2] For an argument against the inclusion of a psychological authenticity condition, see Oshana (2005). For my analysis and critique of the authenticity condition, see chapter 4.

[3] See, for example, Meyers (1989) and Mackenzie (2000, 2002).

Constitutively relational theories of autonomy, on the other hand, do not confine the significance of the social to the damage it can do to an agent. These theories attempt to articulate the ways in which an agent's autonomy is directly constrained by her place in social structures. In these theories, social relations may causally contribute to or detract from autonomy, but they also play a constituting role in autonomy.[4] Marina Oshana explains, "Autonomy is a condition of persons constituted in large part by the social relations people find themselves in and by the absence of other social relations. Autonomy is not a phenomenon merely enhanced or lessened by the contingencies of a person's social situation; social relations do not just causally facilitate or impair the exercise of autonomy. Rather, appropriate social relations form an inherent part of what it means to be self-directed" (2006, 49).

Discussions of self-governance, specifically of the competence and authenticity conditions, are generally assumed to be exhausted by considerations of the causally relational.[5] My argument focuses on articulating a constitutively relational condition for self-governance. In section 2.2, I note that self-governance involves both self-constructive activities and self-expressive activities. Self-constructive activities are those activities wherein an agent "sets" her motivational system by determining what she values. Self-expressive activities are those activities wherein an agent attempts to instantiate those values in her life. While both sorts of activities are necessary for self-governance, my focus in this chapter will be on self-expressive activities. I explain the standard account of competence with respect to self-expressive activities and identify two assumptions operating in this account. In section 2.3, I develop an argument for adding a constitutively relational condition to the general account. This condition is important for evaluating situations involving the conjunction of relational properties and systemic injustice. Specifically, I suggest that in these sorts of scenarios we need also a communal competence condition to capture the ways in which an unjust lack of participation by others can limit the scope of an agent's self-expressive

---

[4] Westlund's (2009) constitutively relational view is an exception. For Westlund, "autonomy in choice and action . . . relies (at least in part) on the disposition to hold oneself answerable to external critical perspectives on one's action-guiding commitments" (28). Holding oneself answerable involves entering into dialogical or constitutive relation with others. What matters, crucially, for Westlund, is not whether one is actively in this constitutive relation with others at any given moment but that one has a disposition to be in this relation in response to legitimate challenges from others.

[5] Mackenzie, for example, takes one important difference between self-determination and self-governance to be that "[t]he self-governance dimension of autonomy picks out autonomy conditions . . . that are in some sense internal to the person, whereas the self-determination axis identifies external, structural conditions" (2014, 31).

activities. In section 2.4, I engage literature on epistemic injustice in order further to clarify the communal competence condition and to suggest a connection between epistemic injustice and autonomy. In section 2.5, I consider a possible objection to my analysis and clarify the distinction between self-determination and self-governance.

2.2. Competence Conditions

Self-governance "involves having the skills and capacities necessary to make choices and enact decisions that agree, or cohere with, one's reflectively constituted diachronic practical identity" (Mackenzie 2014, 17). This set of skills and capacities include, for example, rational skills such as the ability to process information and make plans, volitional skills such as freedom from (extreme) weakness of the will, imaginative skills, and social skills.[6] In thinking about the skills needed to meet the competence condition, it is useful to distinguish self-constructive activities from self-expressive activities, although there is overlap in the skills needed for these activities. With respect to self-constructive activities, the competence condition for self-governance specifies the skills needed to participate in the creation of the self, understood as one's diachronic practical identity. These skills are the skills needed competently, for example, to determine what one really cares about and to alter one's value system in response to the self-understanding one gains from new experiences. The skills needed for self-expressive activities, on the other hand, are those skills needed competently to plan one's participation in the world in ways that express or are commensurate with that self.

Let me further elaborate the distinction between self-constructive activities and self-expressive activities in order to clarify the specific aspect of self-governance that concerns me in this chapter. Self-constructive activities are those activities wherein we develop our core desires, values, and beliefs. It is through self-constructive activities that a person comes to value, for example, honesty, community, independence, or certain career goals. It is through our self-constructive activities that we develop our motivational systems and core values. While there are different accounts of the criteria

---

[6] See Meyers (1989, 76–91; 2002, 19), Young (1986), Berofsky (1995), Stoljar (2000), Mackenzie (2000, 2014), and Oshana (2006, 76–86).

some value, belief, or desire must meet in order to count as autonomous for that agent, the autonomy of one's motivational system is a matter of its being in some significant sense "one's own." Factors like coercion, manipulation, and the internalization of oppressive norms are thought to threaten the autonomy of our motivational systems and thereby undermine our self-governance. While I will return in subsequent chapters to an examination of the criteria used to determine the autonomy of one's motivational system, for the sake of the present discussion I assume an agent who has engaged in self-constructive activities in a way that secures the autonomy of that agent's motivational system.

Having values, desires, and beliefs that count as autonomous for an agent, however, is not sufficient for full self-governance. A person's life consists of more than just her motivational system. To be a fully self-governing agent one needs also to be able to make one's core values operative in one's life. It is through what I'm calling self-expressive activities that one seeks to enact one's autonomous values in one's life. In addition to having an autonomous motivational system, self-governing agents also seek to make their values, beliefs, and desires manifest in their lives.

While self-creative and self-expressive activities are both necessary for full self-governance, there can be a gap between one's autonomously developed motivational system and the expression of those values in one's life. This gap is often explored through examples of addictions and phobias. X may genuinely value sobriety, and being sober may for X be an autonomous value, yet due to addiction X may nevertheless drink alcohol or use drugs regularly. Y may value engaging in public forms of protest against injustices yet may not attend any public protests due to agoraphobia. While both X and Y may have autonomous motivational systems, they are not fully self-governing because they cannot bridge the gap between their values and their actions.

While examples of addictions and phobias are useful for illuminating the potential gap between self-creative and self-expressive activities and thus for clarifying the dual nature of achieving self-governance, the complicated medical bases underlying addictions and phobias may obscure the common ways in which there can be a potential gap between self-constructive and self-expressive activities. Suppose that A and B both value patience. For both A and B, this is an autonomously held value. Suppose further that A demonstrates patience in her life. She is aware that she tends toward snap judgments, negativity, and frustration, and she engages in practices to mitigate those tendencies so that her interactions with others actually instantiate the fact that she values patience. B, however, while autonomously valuing patience, does not very often manage actually to be patient. B, for example, has a tendency to interpret hesitation in another as a sign of opposition and rather than being patient reacts with frustration and anger. A enjoys a greater degree of self-governance than B does because A lives her values, while B does not.

My focus in this chapter is specifically on self-expressive activities, on the potential gap between an autonomously held value and the instantiation of that value in an agent's life. This aspect of self-governance is typically discussed through an individualized competence condition. Ultimately, I will argue that when the value under consideration is a relational property and where failures to instantiate that value in a life are due to systemic injustice, we will need a constitutively relational competence condition, a communal competence condition, to understand the nature of the problem for self-governance.

Treatments of self-expressive activities and their relation to self-governance are typically discussed in terms of an (individualized) competence condition which focuses on articulating the set of skills needed to ensure that our attempts to participate in the world in ways reflective of who we are meet a standard of **effectiveness**. Christman claims that "relative to any characteristic C, where C refers to basic organizing values and commitments," a person meets the competence condition for self-governance if "[t]he person is competent effectively to form intentions to act on the basis of C. That is, she enjoys the array of competences (or skills) that are required for her to negotiate socially, bodily, affectively, and cognitively in ways necessary to form effective intentions on the basis of C" (2009, 155).[7]

On Christman's account, one meets the competence condition if one uses the skills relevant effectively to form intentions even if one fails to achieve what one intends. He clarifies, "It must be noted further that the ability to act—successfully and as planned—cannot be what we mean here. I am often prevented from acting or completing my plans because of the happenstance of my surrounding circumstances.... So the competence conditions for autonomy merely refer to the effective ability to form intentions to act but not to complete such actions" (2009, 154–155).

---

[7] Christman includes a second component of the competency condition: "The person has the general capacity to critically reflect on C and other basic motivating elements of her psychic and bodily make-up" (2009, 155). This aspect of the competence condition is focused on what I'm calling "self-constructive activities."

Meyers, who also advances a rich competency-based account of autonomy, holds a similar position. Although she is discussing the question of the relationship between autonomy and happiness, she supports a position similar to Christman's with respect to the relevance of successful activity in the world. She says:

> Unhappiness can arise from various sources, two of which are particularly germane to the issue of autonomy. People can be unhappy with themselves, or they can be unhappy with their position in the world (or both). Unhappiness with one's self is incompatible with autonomy. For such unhappiness stems either from one's failure to become the sort of person one wants to be (failure with respect to self-definition) or from failure to act in accordance with one's authentic self (failure with respect to self-direction).... But unhappiness with one's position in the world is compatible with autonomy. For, rightly or wrongly, the world may be inhospitable to one's true self, and one may lack the power to win it over. (1989, 74)

On this account, while autonomy is threatened by the sorts of unhappiness that arise from failures of self-definition or self-direction, it is not threatened by failures to achieve what one wants due to an inhospitable social environment. On Meyers's account, self-direction is secured through the use of the relevant capacities to plan actions that express one's authentic self and is not undermined by an inhospitable social environment.[8]

---

[8] While Christman focuses on failures to achieve some specific thing, and Meyers focuses more globally on one's position in the world, I believe Meyers's discussion is inclusive of the kinds of failures that concern Christman. Oshana, in response to Meyers's analysis of the relationship between autonomy and happiness, raises worries about the relationship between autonomy and one's position in the world. She says, "Certainly, persons need not be happy with the social relations they occupy if they are to be autonomous.... However, the fact that a person confronts a world that is 'inhospitable to one's true self' where one 'lack[s] the power to win it over' *is* relevant for autonomy" (2006, 66). On Oshana's account, it is relevant to autonomy because "it makes the realization of one's goals more cumbersome" (66). On this formulation the problem appears to be an unacceptable burden on the agent, but Oshana states the difficulty more strongly in what follows: "I may be perfectly content with myself, have no regrets about the kind of person I am, but be deeply dissatisfied with my place in the world for no other reason than that it denies me *de facto* power over my life" (66). Killmister (2015) also identifies threats to autonomy that arise from cases where an agent does not achieve what she intends: "According to External Self-Realization, if an agent intends to A but in fact Bs, she is failing to fully govern herself. One of the paradigmatic ways in which External Self-Realization can be frustrated is through an external agent's intervention in the realization of an intention. For instance, if you have formed an intention to eat a cookie, but I physically prevent you from eating it... then I have frustrated your External Self-Realization. By substituting my will for yours, I have constrained your relation to yourself.... [Y]our ability to issue directives to yourself may remain untouched, but insofar as those directives are blocked from receiving uptake in action, they cannot fully secure your self-governance" (164–165). While Killmister is concerned with cases where

With respect to some sorts of values and plans, this seems like the right answer; failures to achieve what one intends to achieve do not always carry the implication that competence has been undermined. For example, suppose that one of my basic organizing values is to express care for those I love, and I decide to express this care for my brother by baking him a birthday cake. If I prepare the batter and put it in the oven, but there is a power failure and the cake cannot be baked, my intention has been frustrated, but I don't think it's plausible to suggest that this implies a diminishment of autonomy. I have adequately used *my* skills effectively to form an intention to express my care and affection for my brother, but the happenstance of my circumstance (unanticipated power outage) has frustrated my attempt.

There are, however, two assumptions operating in this account that, as I will argue, limit the scope of its relevance to analyzing failures to bridge the gap between an autonomously held value and the instantiation of that value in a life. First, it is assumed that the set of skills needed effectively to form an intention are all skills that belong solely to the individual agent. This would be unproblematic if all the things we want to accomplish are things we can do by ourselves (where the outside world simply furnishes the "material" on which we enact our skills), but the things we want to do are obviously not exhausted by activities of this sort. Many of the things we want to do involve collaboration with others, and this often requires skills in others. Moreover, many of the things we want to achieve are relational properties that are constituted in relation to others.

There are many examples of these sorts of relational properties: one may want to be powerful, a thief, married, a friend, a lover, a boss, trusted, admired, believed, understood, and so on. Some of these relational properties don't require any active skills to be supplied by the other(s) to whom we are relating (powerful, a boss, a thief). I can, for example, achieve the relational property "thief" if I steal from you even if, as is typically the case, you make no contribution at all beyond being the owner of something I take. But the cases that interest me in relation to autonomy and the competence condition are relations one values and wishes to achieve that are constituted in part by what someone else does. For example, if one wants to be married, be friends with, be recognized, be trusted, admired, believed, or understood, the active participation of others is needed in order for our desires for these things to

---

an agent fully has a skill necessary to achieve an intention but is frustrated because another blocks its use, the cases I'm interested in here involve communal skills.

be realized. These traits are not merely supported or potentially thwarted by what others do; they are partially constituted by what others do.

The second limiting assumption underlying the standard view of competence, at least on Christman's articulation, is that the barriers to achieving one's intentions are attributable to the "happenstance" of one's environment. One may form effective intentions, fail to realize what one wants, yet nevertheless meet the competence condition because the barriers are accidental and capricious rather than structural features of the environment. The social environments in which agents attempt to bridge the gap between their autonomously held values and the expression of those values in their lives are not only vulnerable to accidental or haphazard barriers; some of the barriers agents face are systemic injustices and forms of oppression.

2.3. Communal Competence

I want to think through the implications for autonomy and self-expressive activities if we consider cases (a) where what one wants to achieve is a relational property that requires some level of active participation from another/others in order for the property to be constituted and (b) where it is systemic injustice, rather than accidental happenstance, that frustrates an agent's ability to fulfill the desire.

Before proceeding with my argument, let me consider a potential objection to my line of investigation. My focus is on relational traits, traits that require the participation of others for their constitution. One may object, however, that these relational traits are not relevant to autonomy in general or self-governance in particular. More specifically, while actions, intentions, motives, and attitudes can be autonomous, it is not clear that agents ought autonomously to be able to achieve relational properties, and thus centering these types of traits for analysis is misguided.

I think three points are relevant to answering this objection. First, my point is not to evaluate whether valuing these types of traits is autonomous. I have stipulated an agent whose values are autonomous. Second, my point is not to evaluate whether the trait is achieved autonomously or nonautonomously, where "autonomously" tracks something like entirely through one's own power.[9] Instead, my goal is to analyze how we should think about the

---

[9] For example, I am not suggesting that an agent's autonomy may be restricted just in case she fails to have full power and control over achieving something she values. It is not simple dependence on the participation of another that concerns me here.

self-expressive aspect of self-governance in cases involving relational traits.[10] So my specific question concerns the conditions that must be met in order for an agent to exercise the self-expressive aspect of self-governance. My concern is with the question: When does a failure to instantiate a value in one's life reveal something problematic for the self-expressive aspect of self-governance? Third, my reason for including relational, and not just nonrelational traits, in my analysis is that *anything* that can be valued by an agent is relevant to the particular aspect of autonomy I am investigating here. Specifically, what I am concerned about is an account of what is involved in potentially bridging the gap between valuing X and enacting X in one's life. Since we do value relational properties, just as we value nonrelational ones, both are relevant to assessments of potential barriers to bridging the gap between the value and its expression in one's life. To deny this is to assert that the set of things we can autonomously value is exhausted by nonrelational traits. Agents, however, regularly value a wide array of constitutively relational traits, such as being respected, being believed, being trusted, being admired, and being a friend. My concern here is not with the conditions the value must meet in order to count as an autonomous value for an agent. Those conditions are specified by the conditions for self-constructive activities which I will explore in later chapters. For the sake of argument, I am stipulating that the value is autonomous for the agent. My concern is with the bridge between an autonomously held value and the instantiation of that value in an agent's life. So, just as we can examine the conditions required in order for an agent to count as self-governing with respect to bridging the gap between the nonrelational traits she values, such as being honest or being punctual or being kind, and the instantiation of those values in her life, so too we can examine the relevant conditions when it is a constitutively relational trait under investigation.

Since agents regularly do value relational properties and since an agent's ability to form effective intentions to bridge the gap between an autonomously held value and the instantiation of that value in a person's life is relevant to the self-expressive aspect of self-governance, I think we need to alter the standard view of competence. In addition to the standard competence condition, a communal competence condition needs to be added to the standard competence condition. This communal competence condition will describe the competencies, not of the agent, but of those in the social sphere

---

[10] Specifically, my concern is with constitutively relational traits that require some kind of active involvement of another in order for the trait to be constituted.

in which the agent is attempting to enact her autonomously held values. This condition is important as a way to identify structural barriers to agents' self-governance. And this condition captures the precondition under which it makes sense to employ the standard competence condition. More specifically, the standard competence condition does not require achievement of one's goal but distinguishes successful self-governance (in bridging the gap) from unsuccessful self-governance (in bridging the gap) using the standard of whether the agent formed effective or ineffective intentions to bridge the gap. What this condition, on its own, misses, however, is the fact that for marginalized agents, some social circumstances preclude their ability to intend (to instantiate the value) at all. And if an agent cannot intend at all, the question of whether she meets the standard competence condition becomes irrelevant. My proposal, therefore, is that we need to add a communal competence condition along with the standard competence condition in order to capture relevant barriers to an agent's ability to be self-governing.

Consider the following example. L values earning the respect of her colleagues at work, and she understands that in her particular workplace respect is gained on the basis of the quantity and quality of innovative ideas an employee introduces. This value, being respected by her colleagues, depends on what L does (the quantity and quality of her innovative ideas) and partly on what her colleagues do (extend respect when appropriate). Consider the following options for L with respect to bridging the gap between her value (earning respect from her colleagues based on the quality and quantity of her innovative ideas) and achieving that relational property in her work life. In scenario A, L works hard, comes up with an impressive number of innovative ideas, and presents them to her colleagues on numerous occasions. Her colleagues listen to her ideas and give her credit for them. In this scenario, L has formed effective intentions to bridge the gap between the value, the relational property of being respected by her colleagues, and actually instantiating this value in her life. So she has successfully met the standard competence condition. In scenario B, L gives minimal thought ahead of time to the ideas she will present and is in fact not very good at coming up with innovative ideas on the spot. Often she fails to introduce any ideas at all during important projects, or she presents derivative, poorly conceived ideas and gets no uptake from her colleagues. She has forums to present her ideas, but she has not put in the work to make those ideas interesting, articulate, and compelling. In this scenario, L has not formed effective intentions to bridge the gap between her value and its instantiation in her life and thus has not met the standard competence condition.

The standard competence works well in scenarios A and B to evaluate whether L is self-governing with respect to her self-expressive activities. But consider scenario C. L works hard to develop an impressive set of innovative ideas and has the skills to present them in a clear, articulate, and compelling manner. L, however, works in a male-dominated field and finds that whenever she attempts to articulate her ideas, her male colleagues regularly either interrupt her so she can't articulate her ideas in the relevant meetings or they take credit for her ideas. Over time, she becomes aware that the sexist behavior of her male colleagues structures the environment in which she wishes to express her ideas as the means to gaining respect in the workplace. In this social environment, it is not possible for L to gain respect from her colleagues on the basis of their recognition of her innovative ideas because, in this scenario, their sexism prevents them from recognizing that she has ideas at all.

In my view, the significant difference between scenarios A and B, on the one hand, and scenario C, on the other hand, is that in scenario C it is not possible for L to achieve her goal. The sexism of her male colleagues creates a social space where half of the relational property L wishes to achieve is systematically and unjustly withheld: her male colleagues will not recognize that she has ideas to contribute. In the face of her colleagues' sexism, achieving her goal of earning respect from her colleagues on the basis of her innovative ideas is impossible. It is impossible because achieving a relational property is not possible in the absence of all the aspects that constitute the property.[11] The impossibility of achieving her end has implications for L's ability to form intentions to instantiate that end in her life.

The scope of what one can intend to do is narrower than the scope of what one can want, wish for, or desire. One can want, wish for, or desire what is impossible, but one can intend to do only what is possible. This is because what one can intend to do is indexed to the set of things where one's agency matters, where there is something (or some things) the agent

---

[11] One may be skeptical about whether it is accurate to describe the achievement of L's goal as impossible. While it is logically impossible to achieve a relational trait without the necessary components of the relation, perhaps L could engage in educational endeavors to convince her colleagues that their behavior is sexist and cause them to reform so they become receptive to her ideas. I return to and answer this line of objection in section 2.4 of this chapter.

can do potentially to bring about the desired end. One can, for example, intend to get in shape because there are things, such as exercising, eating well, and getting enough rest that an agent can do to bring about this goal. One cannot, however, intend, one can only wish or want, to be immortal because achieving immortality is impossible, and there is nothing an agent can do to contribute to achieving that goal.[12]

In scenarios A and B, L's goal is possible for her to achieve. In scenario A, she chooses to develop and precisely articulate innovative ideas to potentially receptive colleagues. L's goal, earning respect, is possible, and she meets the standard competence condition of intending effectively to instantiate that value in her life. In scenario B, L does not develop innovative ideas or present them well. While her colleagues are potentially receptive to her ideas, L does not choose means to secure their active reception of her ideas and thus earn their respect. In scenario B, although the goal is possible to achieve, L fails the standard competence condition by failing to intend effectively. Scenario C is significantly different; in this context, due to the sexism of her male colleagues, L's goal is impossible to achieve. Because it is impossible for L to achieve her goal in this context, there are no means she could select to bring about the goal. The goal is beyond the scope of her practical agency, and her efforts are irrelevant to bringing about the goal. It makes no difference whether L does or does not come up with innovative ideas which she can clearly explain. What should be something L can intend to do is refigured as something L can merely want, wish for, or desire. This inappropriately narrows the scope of her possible self-governance.

In order to articulate the limitation on self-governance that arises in cases where an agent values a relational property that requires active participation from others but that participation is systematically and unjustly

---

[12] I draw on Aristotle's discussion in *Nicomachean Ethics* III.2–3 to ground the framework I'm employing here. In his discussion of choice and deliberation, which amount to what we have been calling "intention" in the competence condition, Aristotle notes that the scope of things we can want or wish for is broader than the scope of things we can choose or intend to do. We can want or wish for impossible things, like immortality, but we cannot choose or intend to achieve immortality (III.2, 1111b20–21). This is because, he explains, "choice seems to relate to the things that are in our own power" (1111b30). Similarly, in his discussion of deliberation he claims that we cannot deliberate about things that cannot be brought about by our own power; rather "we deliberate about the things that are in our power and can be done" (III.3, 1112a31). The central insight here, I think, is that if the end one desires is something impossible to achieve, then there is no intending (selecting the means) to achieve it because there are no such means available. In cases where the end desired is impossible to achieve, it doesn't make sense to discuss intending effectively or ineffectively, for one cannot intend at all; one can only wish, want, or desire.

withheld, I think we need to add a communal competence condition to the standard, individual competence condition. This condition will describe the competencies, not of the agent, but of those in the social sphere in which the agent is attempting to enact her autonomously held values. When considering the self-expressive aspect of self-governance with respect to relational properties, when we are considering an agent's ability to bridge the gap between an autonomously held relational value and its instantiation in her life, we need to consider two types of competence conditions. First, we need a communal competence condition which determines whether the community in which an agent is attempting to act is competent to support the *possibility* of the agent bridging the gap between her autonomously held value and the instantiation of that value in her life. The community will count as competent when they do not withhold their constituting part of the desired relation due to systemic injustice. When the community fails to meet the communal competence condition, the self-expressive component of an agent's self-governance is inappropriately constrained; the scope of self-governance is narrowed in comparison to those who do not face these injustices. Second, we will also need to employ the standard competence condition which evaluates whether an agent intended effectively or ineffectively to achieve her goal. The standard competence condition, however, will be relevant with respect to relational properties only if the communal competence condition is met. If the communal competence condition is not met, there are no intentions, effective or ineffective, to evaluate using the standard condition.

Let me make a few points of clarification about the proposal. First, the communal competence condition does not require success in bridging the gap between an autonomous value and the instantiation of the value in an agent's life; it only requires that bridging the gap is possible or, to put the point another way, that the set of means that could lead to the goal is not an empty set. Second, the systematic injustice proviso is important. When the instantiation of our values depends on active cooperation from others, we are all vulnerable to limitations; this alone does not inappropriately narrow the scope of one's agency. For example, if I am a megalomaniac and value the relational trait "being revered by all without question," my agency is limited by others' refusal to afford me unquestioning reverence, but my agency is not inappropriately constrained. No one has a claim to expect that kind of participation from others. Likewise, if we are engaged in a philosophical debate and you listen to my arguments, afford me an appropriate amount of epistemic credibility, but simply aren't convinced, the scope of my agency has not been inappropriately constrained by the fact that you don't believe my position to be correct. In these two examples, a person's agency is constrained, but not inappropriately constrained. An inappropriate constraint on the scope of one's self-governance requires a systematic, unjust barrier to possible uptake.

2.4. Communal Competence and Epistemic Injustice

In the previous section, I argued for the addition of a communal competence condition that better describes situations where an agent autonomously values a relational property but cannot bridge the gap between that value as part of her motivational system and the instantiation of that value in her life due to systemic injustice. In particular, I suggested that the scope of her ability to intend is inappropriately narrowed and that we should add a communal competence condition in order to articulate the constraint on self-governance. In this section, I further clarify and illustrate the point by arguing that epistemic injustice functions to narrow the scope of what an agent can intend and that the communal competence condition helps to illuminate the problems for self-governance generated by epistemic injustice.

Discussions of epistemic injustice focus on the systematic constraints members of marginalized groups face on their ability to be believed or understood. "Being believed" and "being understood" (in the sense of one's communicative endeavors being intelligible to another) are two relational properties that fit the confines I'm interested in. I think it is uncontroversial to suggest that, unless there is some mitigating, functionally valuable factor involved, people typically want to be believed and understood in their communicative attempts and that this is an ordinary desire. Moreover, "being believed" and "being understood" are relational properties; one cannot be believed or understood if no one believes or understands. While it is sometimes the case that happenstance frustrates one's attempts to achieve these relational properties, work in social epistemology on the issue of epistemic injustice provides analyses that delineate the structural barriers in the social environment that members of marginalized communities face when attempting to achieve these quite ordinary everyday relations.

Miranda Fricker identifies and explicates two different types of epistemic injustice (injustices that harm one's capacity as a knower): testimonial injustice and hermeneutical injustice.[13] As Fricker explains, "Testimonial injustice occurs when prejudice causes a hearer to give a deflated level of credibility to a speaker's word.... An example ... might be that the police do not believe you because you are black" (2007, 1). In cases of testimonial injustice, a hearer gives a speaker a deflated level of credibility because of prejudice based in the speaker's social identity (race, class, gender, religion, sexual orientation, etc.). This deflated level of credibility is not caused simply by "happenstance" but arises because of identity prejudice, a structural and often predictable feature of the social environment for members of marginalized communities. This systemic feature of the social world can frustrate an agent's attempts to bridge the gap between his value, "being believed," and the manifestation of that value in his life.

Testimonial injustice structures many social spheres in which members of marginalized groups attempt to be believed. A person's everyday, ordinary communicative attempts may be thwarted by testimonial injustice in legal institutions, at work, at school, in one's family, in one's social sphere, in the grocery store, and so on. Members of marginalized groups face quite common and pervasive disbelief when attempting to communicate the basic experiences of their lives; claims of sexual harassment and assault, of racial profiling, of prejudicially driven slights and aggressions are simply not believed. Berenstain sums up the problem as follows: "When marginalized persons offer testimony about their general knowledge or lived experiences of oppression, privileged persons often respond with skepticism about the content of their claims. . . . These responses may include skepticism that the marginalized person's experience happened the way they describe or skepticism that their experience falls within a larger pattern of oppression rather than simply being an isolated or anomalous incident" (2016, 579). Dominantly situated persons, on the other hand, are typically extended credibility when they describe their ordinary, everyday experiences. They are not typically asked an absurd string of skeptical questions, questions which demonstrate that the questioner doubts the person's basic ability accurately to interpret and describe a situation or experience.

Consider the following example that illustrates Fricker's claim that "[t]estimonial injustice occurs when prejudice causes a hearer to give a

---

[13] My focus for now is on testimonial injustice; I will return to hermeneutical injustice later in the discussion. For an alternative discussion of epistemic injustice and autonomy, an account that focuses on how epistemic injustice can damage a person's self-worth and self-knowledge, see Roessler (2015).

deflated level of credibility to a speaker's word. . . . An example . . . might be that the police do not believe you because you are black" (2007, 1). C is a Black man who is stopped by the police while driving to work. He explains to the officer that he is on his way to work and that he is a lawyer. He is dressed in a suit and his briefcase is on the passenger seat. The police officer, however, does not believe him due to testimonial injustice. He extends extremely low credibility to C because he is racist; he believes that Black people are prone to criminality and that well-dressed Black men are not engaged in legitimate business but are very likely to have made their money in criminal drug activity. Due to his epistemic bias, the officer does not give any weight to C's explanation of where he is going. Instead of believing C, he detains him and proceeds thoroughly to search the car. C realizes that nothing he says and no evidence he offers will make a difference to whether the officer believes him or not. His potential efforts to be believed are irrelevant in this situation due to structural prejudices in the officers' attitude toward him.

In my view, C faces not just an epistemic injustice, one that harms him in his status as a knower, but also a constraint on his potential to be self-governing. C values being believed by the officer but is aware that nothing he says or does will contribute to achieving this goal. The possibility of bridging the gap between his value, being believed, and its instantiation in this circumstance is removed from the scope of his agency. Accordingly, his practical efforts are rendered irrelevant—he cannot form an intention but can only want or desire to be believed. In comparison to a white person in the same situation, C's agency, the scope of what he can intend, is truncated. This is not because he fails to achieve his desired end; it is because he cannot intend to achieve his desired end. The constraint on his self-governance, on his ability, potentially, to bridge the gap between his value and the instantiation of this value in his life is due to a failure of the communal competence condition. The police officer, due to his racism, is not competent to support the possibility of C's bridging the gap between his value and its instantiation in this scene because the police officer unjustly withholds his part of the relation—he does not extend an appropriate level of credibility to C.

The second sort of epistemic injustice Fricker examines is hermeneutical injustice; while Fricker's original formulation isn't relevant to my immediate analysis, subsequent treatments by Dotson (2011, 2012), Medina (2013), and Pohlhaus (2012) expand the concept to address cases where hermeneutical resources have been developed but do not gain purchase. In the case of testimonial injustice, what is said is intelligible even though it isn't believed, while in the case of hermeneutical injustice, the intended audience of one's communicative effort fails to comprehend what is being said. Rather than being understood the speaker is misunderstood.

Pohlhaus delineates willful hermeneutical ignorance as a specific type of hermeneutical injustice. Willful hermeneutical ignorance picks out cases where good epistemic resources, as developed by those with the relevant situated experience, are available to a dominant knower, but the dominant knower preemptively dismisses or ignores those resources (2012, 722). Pohlhaus explains:

> We can see this kind of preemptive dismissal, for example, in the reception that ideas like the "situated knower" have received in mainstream epistemology. We also see this happen when those situated dominantly dismiss the viability of . . . arduously honed concepts like "white privilege," "date rape," or "hetero-normativity." These epistemic resources, which could (and sometimes do) help dominantly situated knowers to know the world in light of marginalized situatedness, can be preemptively dismissed, because, attuned to what is not immediately present within the experienced world of the dominantly situated knower, such resources can appear to the dominantly situated knower to attend to nothing at all, or to make something out of nothing. (722)

One common and very pervasive example of this kind of dismissal is the assessment of members of marginalized groups who object to or report on microaggressions and are understood, not as legitimately angry or hurt due to disrespectful or inferiorizing treatment, but as too sensitive.[14] Derald Wing Sue explains, "Microaggressions are the brief and commonplace daily verbal, behavioural, and environmental indignities, whether intentional or unintentional, that communicate hostile, derogatory, or negative racial, gender, sexual-orientation, and religious slights and insults to the target person or group" (2010a, 5).[15] Microaggressions take many forms, such as telling women to smile, complimenting racial minorities on their command of English, asking someone *what* they are or where they're *really* from, deliberately misgendering a person, structuring public forums and spaces on

---

[14] For a discussion of microaggressions and testimonial injustice, see Dotson (2011). For a discussion of microaggressions and hermeneutical injustice, see Medina (2017).

[15] See also Sue et al. (2007) and Sue (2010b). For the original coining of the term "racial microaggressions," Sue points us to the work of Chester Pierce. See Pierce et al. (1978).

the assumption that there are only two genders, mistaking brown people for service staff, and so on.

When a person who has experienced a microaggression (or more typically a series of them) responds with hurt or anger, either to the aggressor or in reporting the incident to others, it is very frequently the case that rather than being understood as legitimately hurt or angry, she is instead misunderstood as overreacting or, more simply, as being too sensitive. While the hermeneutical resources needed to understand why the agent takes the experience to be angering or hurtful or disrespectful (because it expresses hostile, derogative, or negative slights and insults) are available, these resources are not used, and the agent is misunderstood as being "too sensitive," as being angry or hurt over nothing.

Consider the following example. W arrives at a family gathering after a long plane ride. She is angry and frustrated; the man in the seat beside her on the plane indulged in a constant stream of subtly sexist remarks for the duration of the flight. For example, he kept telling her to smile, giving her tips to "improve" her appearance, and asking her to go to dinner with him at the end of the flight. While W told him she wanted to read her book, this man kept up his intrusions. Her trip was full of sexist microaggressions. When she tells her family about the incident as an explanation of why she is angry, they make fun of her for being too sensitive and claim that he was likely just being friendly and trying to pass the time. When W further explains that his intrusions were sexist and unwanted, they dismiss her as being overly sensitive and not sufficiently friendly. W's family refuses to use the relevant epistemic resources required to understand W's reasons for being angry and persist in misunderstanding her as too sensitive and prone to being upset about nothing at all. W realizes that nothing she says will get uptake from her family, that there is nothing she can do or say that will contribute to achieving the understanding she wants. That outcome is beyond her practical control, and she stops trying to explain herself.

Consider another example. X and Y arrive at a faculty meeting, and both want to vent about the experiences they had on the way there. They both want uptake for their frustrating mornings. X is a white man who complains about the jerk who was driving erratically and cut him off on a particularly dangerous stretch of road. Y is a brown woman who complains about racist treatment in the faculty parking lot; when she was parking her car, a white passerby stopped to explain to her that she can't park there because it is the faculty parking lot. X's colleagues believe his story—they accept that someone did cut X off and that X's characterization of this person as a "jerk" is apt. They do not ask him an endless stream of questions about whether perhaps the person didn't really cut him off or whether he is correct to call this person a "jerk"—they believe his story, X gets to vent, and thus he gets some relief from the stresses of his morning. Y's colleagues, however, treat her story with extreme skepticism. They look for and propose a series of explanations that show they do not believe Y's characterization of the incident as racist. While Y simply wants to be believed and extended the kind of credibility X is extended, she ends up in a lengthy debate about racism that is exhausting and further frustrates her. She is not believed, does not get to vent, and gets no relief from the stresses of her morning. The difference between X's and Y's ability (or inability) to bridge the gap between their respective intentions and the instantiation of that value in this particular social scene does not lie in X's intending effectively and Y's intending ineffectively. Instead, the relevant community, the set of colleagues, uses the relevant epistemic resources to understand X's story but do not use them to understand Y's story. Because they use the relevant resources in the case of X, X is set up to intend effectively or ineffectively. But their failure to use them in the case of Y precludes Y's intending at all.

In both of these examples, an agent seeks understanding from others; she wants others to understand why she is upset and angry. There are epistemic resources available to understand the anger of W and Y. But the others in both examples do not use those epistemic resources. Because the others will not use the relevant epistemic resources, the scope of what W and Y can intend to achieve is truncated. The problem is that the others in the social scene fail the communal competence condition. The communities in which W and Y are attempting to instantiate their values withhold their constituting aspect of the desired relation due to systemic injustice.

Before tying together the connections between self-governance, communal competence, and epistemic injustice, let me consider an objection to the analysis so far. One might object that epistemic injustice doesn't really make one's goals impossible; it merely makes them harder to achieve. One might suggest that achieving the relations "believed" and "understood" in contexts of testimonial injustice and willful hermeneutical ignorance is not really impossible, and thus they can in fact be intended if one employs the right strategies. One can achieve them if one uses one's own skills in order to educate the interlocutors in a way that convinces them to extend credibility or use the available but preemptively dismissed hermeneutical resources. On this view, the burden gets shifted back to the agent's use of skills: she can form a communicative intention if she uses a more complex set of skills to achieve the multistep process of changing interlocutors' epistemic stance in ways that then make room for the desired relations.

Although it is possible in some instances to change an interlocutor's epistemic stance through educational encounters, it is in practice often quite difficult to do so. Members of marginalized groups are well aware of the fact that even if they repeat the same things over and over they still rarely get uptake in epistemically unjust social contexts. But even where success is possible through a multistep educational process, there is a significant difference between what a marginalized agent and a dominantly situated agent can intend. Doing the work required to change the interlocutor into someone who can/will believe or understand typically involves epistemic exploitation. Berenstain explains, "Epistemic exploitation occurs when privileged persons compel marginalized persons to provide an education or an explanation about the nature of the oppression they face. Epistemic exploitation is a variety of epistemic oppression marked by unrecognized, uncompensated, emotionally taxing, coerced epistemic labour" (2016, 570). As I pointed out above, engaging in this work is often ineffective, but should one attempt it the nature of the original desire is altered. One cannot, in this instance, simply intend to be believed or understood; more complexly, one has to allow oneself to be epistemically exploited in the service of the ends of being believed and understood. This is problematic for at least two reasons. First, agents in these situations will face a double bind in which they must choose between allowing themselves to be epistemically exploited as a means to achieving their goal or refusing to be epistemically exploited at the expense of their goal. This double bind identifies a significant difference between what marginalized and nonmarginalized subjects can intend. The former must engage in multistep endeavors that involve their own exploitation, while the latter can directly attempt to achieve their goals. Second, it will also be the case that engaging interlocutors in a way that allows oneself to be epistemically exploited will in many cases undermine the reason one valued the relational trait in the first place. Recall the cases of C and of Y. C wants to be believed by the police officer so that he can get to work on time. Attempting to educate the police officer about his racism is not only dangerous but also incompatible with the reason C wants to be believed in the first place; he wants to be released from the traffic stop in a timely matter so he can get to work. Y wants to be understood by her colleagues as a way of venting about and thus relieving some of the pressure arising from the racist incident she experienced in the faculty parking lot. To take on the difficult project of allowing herself to be epistemically exploited in educating her colleagues certainly does not contribute to her goal of being understood as a mechanism for venting or relieving pressure.

With respect to wanting to be believed or understood, the scope of what members of marginalized groups can intend is narrowed in contexts marked by the relevant kinds of epistemic injustice. My point is both logical and practical. It is logically impossible to achieve a relation without all of the relevant relata. It is impossible, for example, to be married to no one (although one may of course be unmarried), and it is impossible to be trusted with a secret if no secret is shared. Similarly it is impossible to be believed by Z if Z will not extend the credibility required for belief, and it is impossible to be understood by Z if Z will not employ the hermeneutical resources required to enable understanding. Because this is logically impossible, it is impossible for everyone; it is beyond the scope of everyone's agency. This, in itself, is no threat to autonomy.

Practically speaking, however, a problem for autonomy arises. Testimonial injustice and willful hermeneutical ignorance are pervasive and structure many social domains. Because they function to withhold the presence of the relata required for achieving the relational properties believed and understood, members of marginalized groups will often find themselves in social domains where they cannot form intentions to achieve these ordinary aspects of life, aspects of life that members of dominantly situated groups can intend to achieve in most social domains. Dotson captures both the logical and the practical point: "[T]o communicate *we all need an audience willing and capable of hearing us.* The extent to which entire populations of people can be denied this kind of linguistic reciprocation as a matter of course institutes epistemic violence" (2011, 238). My suggestion is that this sort of epistemic violence also constitutes a constraint on autonomy. To live in a world where one frequently cannot intend to achieve such ordinary desires is a constraint on autonomy because it problematically narrows the scope of one's practical agency. Relations that are within the scope of agency for the dominantly situated are removed from that scope for marginalized subjects. The problem is not that the agent *fails* to be self-governing but that the conditions for participating in the activities through which self-governance is secured, specifically intending to act in ways that express or cohere with one's practical identity, are precluded from the context. One's self-governance is effected in these contexts not because one *fails effectively* to intend, but because one cannot intend at all. This is a constraint on the appropriate scope of one's self-governance.

My proposed communal competence condition captures the nature of the restraint on self-expressive activities for agents that value being believed and/or understood in social scenes marked by epistemic injustice. In order for an agent potentially to bridge the gap between her value, being believed and/or being understood, and the instantiation of that value in a particular social context, the participation of others in that context is required. The nature of the participation required is captured by the communal competence condition, which determines whether the community in which an agent is attempting to act is competent to support the *possibility* of the agent's bridging the gap between her autonomously held value and the instantiation of that value in her life. In the epistemic injustice examples, the community will count as competent when they do not withhold their constituting parts of the desired relations due to epistemic injustice. They will count as incompetent, however, if they fail to extend an appropriate level of credibility (in the case of testimonial injustice) or fail to employ the relevant epistemic resources (in the case of willful hermeneutical ignorance) due to epistemic injustice. When the community fails to meet the communal competence condition, the self-expressive component of an agent's self-governance is inappropriately constrained; the scope of self-governance in narrowed in comparison to those who do not face these injustices.

2.5. Concluding Thoughts

My point in this chapter has been to identify a potential constraint on the self-expressive aspect of self-governance and to articulate a condition that can capture the nature of this constraint. The self-governance axis of autonomy includes both (a) a creative or constructive aspect whereby one relies on skills relevant to self-knowledge in order to participate in the fashioning of one's diachronic practical identity and (b) an expressive aspect whereby one attempts to participate in the world in ways that reflect or are commensurate with that identity.

Sometimes, however, one is unable to bridge the gap between an autonomously held value and the instantiation of that value in one's life. On standard accounts of the competence condition, such failures are either

(a) irrelevant to an agent's autonomy: she used the relevant skills, formed effective intentions, but was simply thwarted in her attempts to enact those intentions; or (b) relevant to an agent's autonomy because although she intended to X, her intention failed to meet the standard of being an effective intention. On this view, oppressive social conditions are relevant to self-governance when they play a causal role in accounting for why an agent does not have or does not use the skills relevant to forming effective intentions. Oppressive, unjust social environments may be the cause when an agent lacks the skills to enact the possible path between a value and the instantiation of that value or has the skills but does not feel entitled to use them. For example, consider an agent who values clearly and directly expressing her emotions. If this agent has been socialized, as many girls are, to translate angry responses into sad responses, she may not have the skills to articulate her anger and may instead communicate that she is sad.[16] Alternatively, this agent may have the skills to understand herself as angry yet refrain from using them because she fears the consequences of expressing her anger.

What I'm suggesting is that there is an additional way in which unjust social relations are relevant to an agent's ability to bridge the gap between an autonomously held value and the instantiation of that value in her life. Failures to achieve what one wants are relevant to autonomy when an agent is prevented from forming an intention to fulfill a desire for an ordinary relational property due to an unjust, systemically supported lack of skills in others. To return to the previous example, an agent may both have the skills to understand that she is angry and not be constrained by fear of using those skills, but have no path to the communication of anger because the community in which she is attempting to act does not have the skills to understand women's anger. When the community in which the agent is attempting to act does not meet the communal competence condition, when the community withholds their constituting part of the desired relation due to systemic injustice, the self-expressive aspect of self-governance is inappropriately constrained. Autonomy is diminished because the agent cannot intend to do perfectly ordinary things, things those unaffected by systemic injustice take for granted. In these cases, social relations play a constitutive role; they partially constitute whether it is possible for an agent to bridge the gap between her value and the instantiation of that value in her life. When the communal

---

[16] For recent examinations of women and anger, see, for example, Chemaly (2018) and Cooper (2018).

competence condition is not met, self-governance is constrained because the practices through which self-governance is possible for an agent are inappropriately truncated.

Let me end this chapter by addressing a potential objection to my analysis. One may object that the constraint on autonomy, in cases where the communal competence condition is not met, is really a constraint on self-determination and not on self-governance. Self-determination "involves having the freedom and opportunities to make and enact choices of practical import to one's life" (Mackenzie 2014, 17). Self-determination is constrained when agents lack appropriate freedom and opportunity conditions. So, on the objector's view, the problem with unjust social situations that render some social-relational properties beyond the scope of someone's agency is that this person faces diminished opportunities relative to those who do not face those constraints.

I think there is some merit to this objection. I agree with the objector that agents in the situations I've been describing face constraint on their self-determination because they do not have the range of opportunities that nonmarginalized agents have. They lack the appropriate opportunities to be fully self-determining. I think, however, that constraints on self-determination can also, when they intersect with an agent's values, be constraints on self-governance.

Self-determination tracks constraints on opportunities and freedoms that an agent faces. Constraints on self-determination are constraints independently of what a particular agent values. A person who is incarcerated, whose schedule is almost entirely dictated by external forces, lacks full self-determination even if this particular agent is not bothered by the imposed schedule. Self-governance, however, is intrinsically tied to what an agent values. This means that if we have two agents who are both constrained with respect to their self-determination, they may nevertheless differ with respect to the question of whether they are also constrained in their self-governance. The difference between the person who is merely constrained with respect to self-determination and the person who is constrained with respect to both self-determination and self-governance is located in a difference in the values of these two people.

Let's return to the example of L above. I have argued that in scenario C, the scope of L's self-governance is inappropriately narrowed because the sexism of her colleagues precludes the possibility of her gaining respect on the basis of her innovative ideas. Imagine another agent, M, in the same situation.

M does not value being respected by her colleagues on the basis of her innovative ideas. She hates the job, is doing it exclusively for financial reasons, takes no personal satisfaction in the job, and is indifferent to how her colleagues regard her. In both situations, their colleagues fail to meet the communal competence condition. For both L and M, this constitutes a constraint on their ability to be self-determining. They both lack the opportunity to earn respect in this context. But, on my view, L is and M is not additionally constrained with respect to self-governance. The reason L is additionally constrained, while M is not, is because self-governance, specifically the self-expressive aspect, is indexed to an agent's particular values. Since M does not value earning the respect of her colleagues, the question of whether she can engage in activities relevant to bridging the gap between her (autonomously held) value and the instantiation in her life does not come up. The constraint on M's self-determination does not affect her ability to be self-governing because being respected by her colleagues is not within the sphere of things she cares about. For L, however, being respected by her colleagues is something she values, and thus bridging the gap between that value and its instantiation in her life does matter to L's ability to be self-governing.

Claiming that L is additionally affected in her self-governance while M is not reveals also something significant about the relationship between the self-determination axis of autonomy and the self-governance axis of autonomy. Constraints on self-determination track factual constraints on freedoms and opportunities. Identifying these constraints allows an articulation of the nature of the social world that an agent faces. These constraints are constraints independent of an agent's values (and they do not require an agent to value in any particular way). Constraints that are articulated in relation to an agent's ability to be self-determining do not require that an agent value what is blocked by the constraint. There is, however, a significant difference in terms of autonomy attribution between an agent who does not value and an agent who does value what is blocked by the constraint on self-determination. The agent who does value what is blocked by the constraint on self-determination has her autonomy further diminished. This is not because she has more factual constraints on what she can do, but because she has a different relation to some of those constraints. Because she values what is blocked by the constraint, an additional dimension of her autonomy is affected. A constraint on self-determination, when it intersects with an agent's values, also constrains the self-expressive aspect of self-governance.

The communal competence condition I have proposed captures the nature of this additional constrain. When an agent values a relational property, two conditions are relevant to determining whether this agent is self-governing with respect to her self-expressive activities, with her attempts to instantiate that value in her life. First, the communal competence condition is needed in order to determine whether self-expressive activities with respect to that value are possible. If the community in which the agent is attempting to instantiate her value does not meet the communal competence condition, if they withhold their constituting part of the desired relation due to systemic injustice, then it becomes impossible for the agent to bridge the gap between her value and the instantiation of that value in her life. The scope of her agency is truncated because she is constrained in the scope of what she can intend to achieve. In these cases, an agent does not fail to be self-governing; she is prevented from being self-governing. Second, the standard competence condition, which considers whether an agent intends effectively or not, will be relevant in those cases where the communal competence condition is met. It will then be appropriate to evaluate whether an agent's intentions meet a standard of effectiveness. If, however, the communal competence condition is not met, this second condition will be irrelevant because there are no intentions to evaluate.

3
Self-Governance, Hermeneutical Resources, and Communicative Needs

3.1. Introduction

Self-governance involves meeting a competence condition which has both a self-expressive and a self-creative aspect. In the previous chapter, I argued that competence with respect to self-expressive activities should be rendered communally rather than exclusively as an individualistic feature of an agent. In this chapter, I turn to an examination of the relationship between socially available hermeneutical resources and the self-creative aspect of self-governance.

Agents seeking to live autonomous lives must frequently consider and revise their identity in light of new experiences and situations. A self-governing agent must not only be able effectively to form intentions to act on the basis of her values and commitments but must also possess and exercise the skills that facilitate self-understanding and self-definition so that she can shape her practical identity over time. One must, that is, not only be competent to attempt to enact oneself in the world; one must also be competent to shape that self.[1] This is not a static, one-time accomplishment. Self-governing agents understand themselves, commit to who they want to be, and revise their self-conceptions over time in response to the things they do, the things they learn, and the things that happen to them.

Self-understanding and self-definition require the use of a range of agential skills and the availability of a rich set of hermeneutical resources. Coming to understand and redefine oneself in response to new experiences involves drawing on the contextually available interpretive resources about the possible meanings of our experiences. Sometimes, however, one faces

---

[1] The question of the relationship between self-creative activities and authenticity is complicated; I address authenticity in chapter 4.

barriers to self-understanding, not because one lacks the necessary agential skills but because the hermeneutical resources required to make sense of one's experiences are unavailable.

Édouard Louis's (2018) autobiographical novel, *History of Violence*, provides a rich account of an agent attempting to gain self-understanding and revise his identity in a situation where he is without adequate hermeneutical resources. In this novel, we find an agent (the main character Édouard) who wants to gain self-knowledge and revise his diachronic practical identity after a traumatic and violent encounter, but whose attempts are frustrated by the inadequacies of the hermeneutical resources available to him and by the ways in which his interlocutors engage his communicative attempts.

I engage Louis's novel in order to bring into focus three points of connection between autonomy and the availability of adequate hermeneutical resources. First, I consider how the self-creative aspect of self-governance can be stymied when the available hermeneutical resources are inadequate for interpreting one's experiences. I argue that adequate hermeneutical resources are important not only for an agent's continued motivation toward self-understanding and self-definition but also because they provide the materials out of which self-understanding and self-definition are constituted. I suggest that the significance of a lack of such resources is best understood according to a model of nested constitution. Second, I examine Édouard's response to the unavailability of the hermeneutical resources needed to make sense of his experiences and argue that his response expresses a communicative need. This communicative need centers the social dimensions of self-understanding and self-definition in situations of hermeneutical inadequacy. Finally, I draw on some of Édouard's attempts to fulfill this communicative need in order to articulate two ways in which communicative exchanges fail and thus fail to meet the needs of agents who are attempting to deepen the available hermeneutical resources through communication with others. In particular, I suggest that attempts to deepen the hermeneutical resources needed for self-understanding and self-definition flounder in contexts where one's words are instrumentalized for extraneous purposes or where one's communicative attempts are mired in sets of historical miscommunications about one's identity. I suggest that these failed attempts at communication trace patterns of failed relationality that constrain self-governance.

3.2. Hermeneutical Resources and Nested Constitution

The self-creative aspect of autonomy competence relies on one's ability both to understand oneself and to define oneself. Self-understanding and self-definition are complicated; while one is never entirely transparent to oneself, there remains a threshold of understanding, broadly construed to include various ways of understanding the self, necessary to autonomy. Furthermore, while self-understanding and self-definition are not accomplished through solitary introspection, they do require active attention and participation on the part of the agent. One must employ a coordinated set of agential skills that bring together, for example, reason, affect, imagination, and interpretation. Meyers provides an insightful account of the interplay of skills needed. In cases, for example, "[w]hen formal decision rules are inapplicable, people are obliged to advert to their inclinations and feelings. They must rely on affective cues—such as frustration or gratification and shame or pride—to guide their judgments" (1989, 79). Moreover, in order to gain understanding of these affective cues, further faculties are needed. Meyers suggests that one will also need to bring "memory, imagination, verbal communication, reason, and volition—into the self-reading process" (79).

In addition to the use of an array of agential skills, agents must also rely on the communal resources available to them. Agents are embedded in particular sociohistorical communities, and the materials needed for self-understanding and self-definition are drawn from these communities. The way that experiences are gendered in the larger culture, for example, will matter to whether one understands oneself to be rebelling against a norm or embracing it or transforming it. Representations of expected behavior along social identity lines will influence what certain experiences "should mean" or "can mean." Norms and expectations can strongly encourage individuals to understand and define themselves in particular ways.

There have been many different accounts of how one's social contexts, with their particular resources, norms, encouragements, and coercions, can matter to one's autonomy. One's context and socialization may withhold the resources one needs to develop or exercise some of one's agential skills (Meyers 2002, 20). One's particular social embeddedness may shape one's preferences around the internalization of false and oppressive norms (Stoljar 2000) or cause an agent to fail to value what one *really* has reason to value, such as an interest in one's own flourishing (Babbitt 1993). One's social context may undermine the self-reflexive attitudes such as self-respect, self-trust, and self-esteem (Anderson and Honneth 2005) or of self-worth (Mackenzie 2000; Charles 2010). Social context may also undermine an agent's desire or ability to take ownership of who they are and what they do (Benson 2005b; Westlund 2009). Less attention, however, has been devoted to articulating the ways in which a lack of socially developed and constituted hermeneutical resources matter to self-creative activities. Louis's autobiographical novel, *History of Violence*, provides material with which to think through the interplay between self-creative activities, agential competencies, hermeneutical resources, and communicative attempts.

History of Violence provides a nuanced account of an agent attempting to gain self-understanding and revise his identity in a situation where he is without adequate hermeneutical resources. In this novel, we find an agent who wants to gain self-knowledge and revise his diachronic practical identity after a traumatic event. Édouard is a twenty-year-old student who has left his small, impoverished, homophobic, gender-rigid village (as is detailed in Louis's earlier autobiographical novel, *The End of Eddy*) and is engaged in building an artistic, intellectually oriented, queer life for himself in Paris.[2] On Christmas Eve, he joins two close friends for a warm and joyous celebration. On his way home, he encounters a man, Reda, who attempts to pick him up for a sexual encounter. While initially he is committed to going home alone to read the books he's been gifted, he eventually invites Reda up to his apartment for sex.

They spend the night together, and Édouard later describes it as being complex: full of laughter, forms of gentleness, mutual fear as someone approaches and tries to enter the apartment, and sexual excitement. At a certain point, however, everything changes in a confrontation over Reda's attempt to steal Édouard's iPad and phone. Édouard becomes obsessed with getting the phone back, things escalate, and Reda becomes increasingly loud and violent. He strangles Édouard with a scarf and eventually rapes him at gunpoint.

The novel is structured around Édouard's repeated attempts to interpret both what happened to him and how he acted. He wants to understand his experience (part of which was a vicious attack, although that aspect of the evening does not exhaust what he wants to think about). His attempts to gain self-understanding and determine how to revise his diachronic practical identity cause a form of manic bewilderment in Édouard because the

---

[2] See Louis (2017).

hermeneutical resources necessary to facilitate self-understanding are inadequate.[3] As the novel progresses, Édouard becomes increasingly catatonic and loses track of his sense of self and of the values that used to motivate him and ground his identity. He becomes "other" to himself. He says, "A second person took over my body; he thought for me, he spoke for me, he trembled for me, he was afraid for me, he inflicted his fear on me, he made me tremble over terrors of his own" (Louis 2018, 199–200).[4]

While the depth and types of hermeneutical resources a person needs in order to achieve self-understanding cannot be universally determined because of the particularity of each individual, the shape of the lack Édouard experiences, and which I think is a commonly encountered kind of lack people face when they have significant experiences, is roughly specifiable at the intersection of important but generic resources and the particularities of the self. The novel opens with Édouard referencing the police report he keeps folded in his drawer, which refers to his experience with Reda as "the attempted homicide." Édouard says that he also calls it "the attempted homicide" "for lack of a better word, since no other term is more appropriate for what happened, which means I always have the anxious nagging feeling that my story, whether told by me or by whomever else, begins with a falsehood" (Louis 2018, 1–2). The conjunction of "no other term is more appropriate

---

[3] In *Aftermath: Violence and the Remaking of a Self*, Brison argues for the crucial role empathetic listeners play in responses to trauma. She centers for analysis the experience of survivors of trauma who "frequently remark that they are not the same people they were before they were traumatized" (2002, 38) and develops a relational account of the self as "both autonomous and socially dependent, vulnerable enough to be undone by violence and yet resilient enough to be reconstructed with the help of empathic others" (38). My point in emphasizing the hermeneutical lack Édouard experiences is not to suggest that he needs hermeneutical resources *instead of empathy*. On Brison's view, an integral part of the value of empathetic listeners is epistemological. Empathetic listeners, for Brison, play many roles, including providing care, support, and sympathy; helping one to gain mastery over the trauma; helping survivors to reconnect with their subjectivity and with their emotions; and bearing witness by listening and believing. Empathetic listeners, as well, are crucial in the process of meaning construction because our self-understandings are developed and framed in terms of social meanings. Brison explains that trauma "unravels whatever meaning we've found and woven ourselves into," but survivors can remake the self in relation to empathic others (58). Empathic others are crucial to the remaking of the self because "[t]o a large extent, we're the keepers of each other's stories, and the shape of these stories has unfolded in part from our interwoven accounts. Human beings don't only search for meanings, they are themselves units of meanings; but we can mean something only within the fabric of larger significations" (Hoffman 1989, 279, as quoted in Brison 2002, 58). While Édouard has friends who listen to him and provide emotional and practical support, the novel is structured around his need for self-understanding and the insufficiency of the hermeneutical resources he has available to interpret and reconstitute his sense of self.

[4] While this description of what has happened to Édouard describes a multifaceted problem for his self-identity, this particular passage describes a conflict between his antiracist values and who he has become. He says, "I had become a racist. Suddenly I was full of racism—the one thing I had always considered most alien, most 'other' to my mind. Now I became one of those others" (Louis 2018, 199).

for what happened" and "I always have the anxious nagging feeling that my story, whether told by me or by whomever else, begins with a falsehood" is revealing of the nature of the hermeneutical lack.

Édouard has available some hermeneutical resources which he views as inadequate yet nevertheless "most appropriate." Fricker's concept of a hermeneutical lacuna is instructive here. Fricker explains that "the extant collective hermeneutical resources can have a lacuna where the name of a distinctive social experience should be" (2007, 150–151). Édouard is not caught in a hermeneutical gap in this technical sense. There are available hermeneutical resources to articulate the distinctive social experiences he has endured—"rape," "strangulation," and "attempted homicide" pick out distinctive social experiences, but at a very general level. While these hermeneutical resources are useful, especially for navigating the legal and medical landscape, and while they do help to identify shared distinctive social experiences, they are not adequate for Édouard's understanding of himself and his attempts to revise his identity. The ability to understand oneself in the ways relevant to autonomy requires more than these important but ultimately generic resources. Epistemic resources that name distinctive social experiences at a generic level are very important to self-knowledge, but they are not sufficient precisely because they are not designed to capture the specific and different meanings of these distinctive social experiences for the individuals who experience them. These sorts of meanings, because they are particular (although not private), need to be worked out within the epistemic communities available to one. A person needs, that is, resources for interpreting what it means for that particular person, with his temperament, background, psychological profile, concerns, imaginings, hopes, and values, to experience X. For example, the term "marriage" picks out a distinctive social experience, but an agent who simply understands herself as married does not have sufficient self-knowledge. She needs also to know, at least in a rough way, what it means for her identity to participate in this distinctive social experience. Has, for example, being married been a long-standing dream of hers? How invested is she in the institution of marriage? Did she marry because it mattered deeply to her, or as a cheerful concession to her partner to whom it mattered? Did she marry for love or for economic and other practical considerations? These types of questions and the resources to answer them are significant to the self-knowledge needed for autonomy because distinctive social experiences which are named by generic hermeneutical resources are experienced by particular selves.

In addition to the important but generic hermeneutical resources available to Édouard, he needs also resources that will allow him to connect the traumatic events he experienced to who he was before the events, how they altered that self, and how they fit together into a new self. For example, Édouard came to Paris, at least in part, to escape the pervasive masculine violence that marked the social context of his childhood and to construct a life where he is free to be queer. While this life trajectory and his vision of himself as escaping masculine violence is interrupted in a significant way by his violent encounter with Reda, the effects on his understanding of his identity reverberate throughout his life. One marked and painful place of reverberation concerns his relationship with two very close friends, Didier and Geoffroy. These two men are sources of joy, comfort, safety, and intellectual companionship in Édouard's life. They tend to and take care of Édouard after the attack, but their friendship and its place and value in Édouard's life becomes fraught with tension around the question of whether Édouard will report the attack to the police. Édouard is vehemently anti-incarceration. His experiences growing up allowed him to see firsthand the horrible effects of incarceration, and it is an important part of his identity that he not go to the police to report the attack. His friends, however, come from a radically different perspective and expect Édouard to involve the police as a way to reduce the risk from Reda to other queer people (Louis 2018, 169–174). In the days following the attack, values that are deeply ingrained in Édouard from his class background and particular experiences come into conflict with the values not only of his new queer community generally but of his dearest friends. With respect to his friends' persistent attempts to convince him to file a police report, he says, "Didier and Geoffroy kept talking, only now I couldn't understand what they were saying, I was so furious I couldn't even see them, I only felt them as admonitory shadows beside me; they were no longer Didier and Geoffroy, they were no longer the two people who had saved my life so many times; those two had ceased to exist" (172). Despite deeply ingrained and visceral anti-incarceration commitments, he is convinced by his friends to go to the police. He has not given up the values he had prior to the attack but finds himself under pressure from his community and does eventually go to the police. Who he is, what his genuine values are, who these friends are to him, and what it means for his identity that he went to the police all trouble Édouard deeply. He says, "At the end of the meal, we paid and we walked toward the police station, but my body was not my own, I watched it lead me there" (174). While this is just one example of the many multifaceted interpretive dilemmas Édouard faces, it emphasizes his need for hermeneutical resources that are adequate for interpreting his experiences of what "rape," "strangulation," and "attempted homicide" mean specifically for his identity, his life, and his self-understanding.

The lack of hermeneutical resources available to Édouard is similar to, although broader than, Mackenzie's account of the importance of a rich cultural imaginary. Mackenzie provides a compelling account of how imagination plays a critical role in self-knowledge and self-definition. She examines the question "[H]ow can a person's imaginative projects, and hence her capacity for self-transformation and autonomy, be stymied by the dominant cultural imaginary?" (2000, 139). Mackenzie treats the presence or absence of appropriate resources in the cultural imaginary as a matter of the presence or absence of social recognition and identifies two ways in which social recognition is crucial to autonomy. She suggests, first, that self-definition depends on self-knowledge and that "we achieve self-knowledge in social relationships" (140). For example, "[o]ur emotional responses to aspects of our identity . . . are shaped by and responsive to the estimations and responses of others" (140). Second, she argues that a sense of self-worth is necessary to self-definition and that self-worth depends on social recognition (140). A severe enough lack of social recognition can undermine one's sense of self-worth which is necessary to motivate one to engage in the difficult task of self-definition (140).[5]

While Mackenzie identifies important ways in which cultural imaginaries matter to self-understanding and self-definition, Édouard's situation clarifies an additional way in which a paucity of hermeneutical resources constrains self-governance. One's self-knowledge may remain empty or suspended with respect to some experiences because the materials (hermeneutical resources) from which self-knowledge is constituted simply do not exist. In order for Édouard to interpret himself and gain self-knowledge, he needs a rich set of hermeneutical resources; this set, however, is unavailable to him. His self-knowledge is constituted (content-wise) from the available hermeneutical resources. In the absence of these resources his self-knowledge is

---

[5] Mackenzie further elaborates "the interconnections among the cultural imaginary, an agent's imaginative projections, and the impairment of autonomy in oppressive social contexts" (2000, 143). The available cultural repertoire is what we draw on in our own imaginative activities; this repertoire can be restrictive and constraining, and it can motivate us to identify with those representations, even if oppressive, that afford social recognition (143–144). Édouard's difficulty is focused on a slightly different problem: there is a lack of relevant hermeneutical resources available in the cultural imaginary.

stymied, and thus he cannot engage in the self-creative activities that rely on this self-knowledge.

It is not that a lack of resources merely causes there to be a lack of self-knowledge by undermining his sense of self-worth and thus his motivation. Édouard in fact remains highly motivated. Rather the material out of which self-knowledge is constituted is nonexistent. Or, to put the point slightly differently, in this case what causes a lack of self-knowledge and thus stymies his self-creative activities is that the constituents needed for self-knowledge (hermeneutical resources) are unavailable. Social resources, in this case, have a ripple effect of suspension of agency in some sphere: a lack of material for self-understanding puts on hold not only self-understanding but also self-definition and thus halts one's self-creative activities.[6] What is important to note, here, is that the chain of causes is grounded not necessarily in damage done to self-worth or in a lack of motivation but rather in the absence of the materials needed for self-understanding.

It is useful, I think, to understand the truncation of self-governance as a problem of nested constitution. A lack of resources causes a lack of self-understanding, which stalls self-definition, which causes a cessation of self-creative activities, which undermines self-governance. The nature of this causal link, however, requires clarification. The causal nature of the relation is one of constitution; each step in the process is partially constituted by material from the previous step. Hermeneutical resources are that from which self-understanding is developed, and self-definition is constituted out of what one understands about oneself; these together provide the material for self-creative activities, which in turn are that from which self-governance is partially constituted.

3.3. Communicative Needs

Agents who face a paucity of hermeneutical resources with respect to significant aspects of their experiences are, as I argued in the previous section, stymied in their attempts to gain self-understanding because the materials out of which such understanding is at least partially constituted are unavailable. Édouard's response to the inadequacy of the materials available to him

---

[6] This can also halt self-expressive activities because there is nothing to attempt to express when one's self-creative activities are hampered.

illustrates a second way in which one may be dependent upon others for the task of self-definition.

Édouard responds to the paucity of resources needed to render his experience intelligible with a communicative need. The absence of the hermeneutical resources required for him to gain self-understanding and assign significance to his experience leaves him alone to do a task that cannot be done alone. He attempts to remedy his aloneness by engaging others. In the days following his encounter with Reda, Édouard experiences an intense need to talk with others about what happened to him. Immediately after the attack, he takes his sheets to wash at the laundromat. He says, "The manager of the laundromat was on duty, his blocky chest and head looming up across the rows of machines. He asked how it was going, I said Bad, in the hardest voice I could muster. I waited for him to say something. I wanted him to say something. But he let it go, he shrugged, he turned and disappeared into the little office of his, tucked away behind the dryers, and I hated him for not asking what I meant" (Louis 2018, 4–5). More generally he says:

> On my calmer days I imagined going up to a stranger in some public place, on the street or in the aisles of a supermarket, and telling the entire story from beginning to end. The way I imagined it, I would walk up, the stranger would be startled, and I'd start talking, as casually as if I'd known him all my life, without ever saying my name, and what I'd tell him would be so ugly he'd have no choice but to stand there and listen till the end; he would listen, and I would watch his face. I spent my time dreaming up scenes where I did this. I didn't tell Clara, but this fantasy of utter shamelessness and self-exposure sustained me for weeks. (25)

Édouard's whole life and sense of self become fixated on understanding his evening with Reda; he is strange to himself and wants to understand how what happened and how he behaved have significance for revising his diachronic practical identity. He rightly understands, however, that the tasks of self-interpretation and coming to understand the significance to his present self are not wholly private. They are social/relational in several ways: they are not private in the sense that he needs support and care, and they are not private in the sense that the skills he has thus far developed for self-knowledge and self-definition were cultivated and sustained with others. But the sense of "not private" that specifically matters for his autonomy, as outlined in section 3.2, is the sense in which interpretation and the assigning of significance rely on the hermeneutical resources contextually available to an agent.

Édouard's potential ability to interpret his experience and fit it meaningfully into his identity depends on hermeneutical resources that will allow him to connect the specific experiences he endured to his particular self. His understanding that interpretive work and the work of assigning significance are not entirely private gives rise in him to a communicative need. Wolfe provides a framework that is useful for understanding Édouard's need. Wolfe explains that while need has historically been conceived of as a wholly negative lack, it should be understood instead as being defined by a vulnerability to harm (2016, 136–137).[7] This account, among other advantages, allows us to distinguish mere desires from needs (137). While we may desire things that do not render us vulnerable to harm should they be left unsatisfied, unsatisfied needs expose us to harm.[8]

Some needs, Wolfe suggests, are relational needs: "Relational needs are needs that arise from interconnections between the self and others and speak to the extent to which fundamental aspects of human well-being have relational dimensions. Needs for such things as recognition, love, friendship, acceptance, respect, and more, number among our fundamental relational needs. As a general rule, moreover, such needs, by virtue of being relational, are needs that one cannot meet oneself" (2016, 131–132). Édouard's intense need to speak, to communicate, should be understood as a relational need. His moving forward as a self-governing agent depends on his ability to revise his self or his diachronic practical identity by assigning significance to what happened to him and to how he acted during his time with Reda. If he cannot do this, then he is vulnerable to the harm of a reduction of autonomy. Moreover, assigning significance is not entirely private but is dependent on what "significances" are available, on what meanings can be contextually supported and generated. His impulse to talk to others about his experience, therefore, should be understood as a relational need.

Édouard understands the potential inherent in communicating with others and thus generating the hermeneutical resources needed. While he

---

[7] For other theorists "who employ a definition of need hinging on the criterion of vulnerability to harm" (Wolfe 2016, 136), Wolfe draws attention to Anscombe (1958), Feinberg (1973), Frankfurt (1988), Rogers, Mackenzie, and Dodds (2012), and Wiggins (1987).

[8] Of course, some of our desires will also be needs.

does not wish to be talking to the police and while, as we will see, his communicative need is not only unmet but actively frustrated, he affirms his communicative need and its potential in his description of his time at the police station. With reference to the police, Édouard says, "I already grasped the importance of their listening. This week... I've noted all the inappropriate and racist remarks the police made, I've noted their complete inability to understand my behaviour, I've noted their obsessions, I've explained everything that separated them from me, everything that made me hate them; at the same time, they helped me in a crucial, decisive way, they represented a place where it was possible for me to say what I had to say, and where this was sayable. From the moment I walked in, they made me feel clearly authorized to speak" (Louis 2018, 83). The potential Édouard sees in the communicative encounter, the potential to deepen the resources available to him, motivates him to engage in the difficult task of working with others to render his experience intelligible.

3.4. Communicative Failures

While communicative encounters with others have the potential of generating the hermeneutical resources Édouard needs to understand his experience, his attempts are thwarted by what others have the power to do with his words. In this section, I consider his attempts to communicate with the police and his attempts to communicate with his sister in order to clarify two sorts of obstacles agents face when attempting to communicate in ways useful to generating the hermeneutical resources required for self-understanding and self-creative activities.

The first communicative context I want to consider is his experience of reporting the incident to the police. His initial appreciation of the police as a representation of a possibility, the possibility of a place where what he has to say is "sayable," not only is disappointed but puts him in a position where he must actively "not say" if he wishes to hold onto his story. The communicative possibility is thwarted by what his interlocutors have the power to do with his words. I focus on two such failures, their racism and their homophobia, both of which reveal an instrumentalization of Édouard's experiences for purposes completely extraneous to his interests.

First, the police engage Édouard's story as a way to indulge their own racist obsessions and for them to bond among themselves. Édouard says:

The copy of the report that I keep at home, drafted in police language, refers to an Arab male. Each time I see that phrase it infuriates me, because I can still hear the racism of the police who interviewed me.... I can hear the compulsive racism that, in the end, seemed the crucial bond between them, the only bond they had ... the only glue that held them together.... At the police station I'd given a brief description of Reda, when they asked, and immediately the officer on duty cut me off: "Oh, you mean he was an Arab." He was triumphant, delighted would be an exaggeration, but he did smile, he crowed; it was as if I'd given him the confession he's wanted to hear since I walked in the door; as if I'd given him proof that he was in the right all along. (Louis 2018, 16–17)

Although Reda is not in fact Arab, Édouard's story gets uptake by his interlocutors because of its instrumental value for his listeners—it provides a way for the police to confirm their prejudices and bond over their racism.

Second, Édouard's attempts to communicate with the police are marked by uncomprehending and judgmental assumptions fueled by homophobia, which ultimately serve to confirm the officers' sense of superior normalcy. In response to Édouard's description of meeting Reda in a quite ordinary and common cruising scene, Édouard describes the following interaction with the officer: "He asked me: 'Wait—you brought a stranger up to your apartment, in the middle of the night?' I answered: 'But everybody does that ...' and in an ironic, mocking sarcastic voice, he said 'Everybody?' It wasn't a question. Obviously, he wasn't asking me whether or not everybody did that, he was saying nobody did that. Or, at least, not everybody. So finally I answered, 'What I mean is, people like me'" (Louis 2018, 48). In this exchange, Édouard's words are once again treated as merely instrumental in a way completely extraneous to anything he needs out of the exchange. His interlocutors use his words to confirm their superior sense of heterosexual and sexual normalcy. The complete instrumentalization of Édouard's words frustrates the communicative possibility and turns him into someone who must instead refrain from speaking. He says:

I no longer recognized what I was saying. I no longer recognized my own memories, when I spoke them out loud; the questions I was being asked by the police made me describe my night with Reda differently than I'd have chosen, and in the form that they imposed on my account, I no longer recognized the outlines of my own experience, I was lost, I knew that once I went forward with the story, according to their cues and directions, I couldn't take it back, and I'd have lost what I wanted to say.... I understood that there were certain scenes, certain things, I must never discuss if I wanted to remember all that had actually happened. (Louis 2018, 89–90)

In this communicative context, Édouard begins by feeling authorized to speak, but his interlocutors use his words in purely instrumental ways, ways that are completely extraneous to any interest Édouard might have in communication. The "significances" available to Édouard in the communicative context are grossly inadequate to his attempts to gain self-understanding and revise his identity. What is available to him in this context is a story in which his experiences are significant only insofar as they can be instrumentalized to shore up the officers' bond over racism and confirm their heterosexual normalcy.[9] Because his interlocutors have the power to put this particular range of possible significance in place, Édouard has to abandon his attempts to communicate, has to keep quiet in order to avoid offering up his whole experience to instrumentalization by others.

In my view, these kinds of instrumentalizing responses frustrate Édouard's autonomy by producing a double bind. On the one hand, as I argued in the previous section, Édouard's ability to achieve self-understanding and revise his practical identity is stymied by the paucity of hermeneutical resources available to him. This lack gives rise to a communicative need. His autonomy depends on deepening the set of hermeneutical resources available to him, and he cannot do this by himself. On the other hand, the instrumentalization of his words effectively silences him. Meyers, drawing on feminist voice theory as developed by Lugones and Spelman (1986), explains that "[s]ilencing disables agency, for the alternative to articulating your own experience and your own goals in your own way is to live someone else's version of you—to inhabit their definition of what you are like and their

---

[9] Peet (2017) identifies a similar phenomenon which he calls interpretive injustice: "Interpretive injustice is the phenomenon whereby a hearer's employment of prejudicial stereotypes results in the hearer attributing a message to the speaker when the speaker never intended to convey that message" (3423). The police attribute to Édouard's story a message he does not intend to convey, but this is not in place of the message Édouard does mean to convey; Édouard lacks appropriate hermeneutical resources and is attempting to engage with the police to produce more adequate resources. It isn't that he intends to convey X but is misinterpreted as saying Y; rather, the heart of the communicative failure is that Édouard needs to communicate for the purpose of A (jointly producing adequate hermeneutical resources), but his words are used for the purpose of B (confirming and supporting the police's racist and heterosexist views).

construal of what you think, feel, and want and consequently to find yourself enacting their story of how your life should go" (Meyers 2002, 16).

While Édouard is not literally silenced in his communicative attempts with the police, their responses push him to engage in what Dotson calls testimonial smothering. Dotson explains that "[t]estimonial smothering, ultimately, is the truncating of one's own testimony in order to insure that the testimony contains only content for which one's audience demonstrates testimonial competence" (2011, 244). While testimonial smothering has many negative epistemological implications, in Édouard's case it also affects his autonomy. In order to avoid having to inhabit the version of himself produced by the testimonial incompetence of the police, he self-silences. But this silencing means that his communicative need not only is left unfilled but is also abandoned, at least in this particular communicative encounter. Édouard is stuck in the bind of either living out someone else's version of himself or having no appropriate version at all; neither option is adequate, and his ability to be self-understanding and self-defining are frustrated.

A second significant attempt to fulfill his communicative need takes place with his sister Clara, and again the potential of the communicative scene is frustrated. Clara is his main interlocutor in the book; the book is mostly structured around her recounting Édouard's story to her husband (with her own commentary and reactions) while Édouard listens from another room and provides commentary and corrections of his own for the reader. This is a rich and nuanced encounter which I cannot do justice to here; what I aim to do is illustrate another type of communicative problem that attends Édouard's attempts to speak.

Specifically, Édouard is trying to make sense of his experiences with Reda, with how he acted then, with what happened, in order to revise his self-conception. His communicative attempt with Clara gets stuck, however, because of Clara's interpretations of Édouard's pre-Reda self, of the self that enters into the scene with Reda. So much accumulates around misinterpretation of Édouard prior to and coming onto the scene that the task of revision cannot happen. What I want to highlight in particular is the way that communicating about his post-Reda self becomes practically impossible because of (a) the struggle for control over interpreting the character of his pre-Reda self and (b) how Clara's false understanding of that self informs her interpretations of Édouard during his time with Reda.

Édouard arrives home to what is a common scene when one has sought to remake oneself outside of the confines of one's upbringing and the expectations of one's family and community, and Édouard feels this very sharply. Speaking of himself in the third person, he reports, "[A]s soon as you arrived she started talking, nonstop, without listening to anything you said, telling you all the trivial gossip of the village, describing all the weddings and funerals of people whose names you don't even remember, as if that way she could give herself the illusion, and give you the illusion, that you'd never left, that these stories still concerned you and that she was picking up a conversation that the two of you had only just abandoned, a day or an hour before" (Louis 2018, 9–10).

From his perspective, Édouard has not just left the village but has actively sought to change himself. In his discussion with Reda, Reda asks why, although he is only twenty years old, he didn't live at home or go to visit for the holidays. Édouard responds:

> I explained that becoming a graduate student was actually a result of my having escaped from my family. The escape came first. The idea of graduate school had only occurred to me later, when I realized that was pretty much the only way I could get away from my past, not just geographically, but symbolically, socially—that is, completely. I could have gone to work in a factory like my brother, three hundred miles from my parents, and never seen them again; that would have been a partial escape. My uncles, my brothers would still have lived inside me: I'd have their vocabulary, their expressions, I'd have eaten the same things, worn the same clothes, I'd have had the same interests. Studying was the only real escape route I could find. (Louis 2018, 80–81)

In response to Édouard's story, as she is recounting it to her husband, Clara reveals her complicated attitude toward who Édouard is: her assessment involves a combination of aesthetic judgment and disdain, a questioning of his motives, and attributions of "unrealness" to his identity. These examples all, to some degree, revolve around the block Clara has against understanding that Édouard's queerness and the aesthetics of that are not confined to who he has sex with but has a more pervasive effect on who he is. In *Queer Phenomenology*, Sarah Ahmed explains as follows: "I would say that being orientated in different ways matters precisely insofar as such orientations shape what bodies do: it is not that the 'object' causes desire, but that in desiring certain objects other things follow. . . . It does 'make a difference' for women to be sexually orientated toward women in a way that is not just about one's relation to an object of desire. In other words, the choice of one's object of desire makes a difference to other things that we do" (2006, 100–101). Matters are complicated by how Édouard's particular queer orientation involves explicit rejections of the norms of his class background. Consider the following two examples which illustrate Clara's general misinterpretation of Édouard's pre-Reda self as it relates to his queerness.

Clara believes that Édouard came out to their family in order to distance them. She misunderstands the situation around Édouard's coming out to his family and attributes motives to him that misrepresent that self, largely because she misinterprets the significance of how the family reacted. She understands (or constructs) the family's reaction as accepting and supportive, while Édouard does not. In the following passage, we find her account and Édouard's response (the italicized parts in parentheses) to her account. She says: "We've always respected him for what he was, always, and when he told us he was different—that very day he told us, I remember like it was yesterday—what did we tell him? We told him it didn't change a thing, we'd love him just the same (*she's lying*), no matter what, and for us he'd still be the same person. We told him all that mattered was his happiness, all we cared about was that he was happy (*she's lying*)" (Louis 2018, 77). Édouard explains that in addition to a childhood of disdain for his too feminine self and a palpable fear that he might be gay, they in fact asked him not to make a big deal of it when he came back to the village because they'd be the ones to pay, told him to keep quiet because his little brother and sister would be picked on at school, asked him not to mince around too much and not to go around in girly clothes, and made him promise not to tell his grandfather (77–78).

On the basis of her understanding of the family's acceptance, Clara resumes her account with a focus on her understanding of Édouard's motives in coming out to the family. She says:

But we accepted him as he was (*not true*). And that's what makes me wonder. That's why the whole thing always leaves me uneasy. Sometimes I think Édouard told us he was different not so we could be closer to him or know him better . . . but actually for the opposite reason. In his heart he didn't want us to accept him. He hoped it would make us push him away, because we'd be hurt and angry that he'd been keeping this secret of his, and we'd reject him, and then afterward he could go and tell everybody, in that stuck-up way he has, You see? It's their fault I'm too cowardly to have a relationship with my family. (Louis 2018, 78–79)

Again, Clara's misinterpretation of what it would mean to be accepting of Édouard pushes her to attribute motives and feelings to Édouard's pre-Reda self that are inaccurate; she mistakenly casts his disappointment and hurt over the family's reaction to him as motivated by his belief that they have rejected him and by his own cowardice and his desire to distance himself from them.

Second, Clara attributes to Édouard an affectation of manner; she thinks that the self he has become is "unreal," that he hasn't really changed, and that his queerness (as larger than just his attraction to men) is an affectation. She says:

> He's changed less than he pretends. I know I'm right. I've seen how he acts when he comes to visit the first few days, when he puts his things in his room and acts so prissy. It's like he's trying to prove he's not one of us, he wants us to think he's different—he wants us to think he's new. That he's too good for us. When he gets here, I think he actually lays it on thicker than when he's with those friends of his . . . back in Paris. I'm sure when he's in Paris and he's feeling relaxed he swishes around less than when he gets here and suddenly won't eat meat . . . or he'll get up and wash his hands every five minutes. . . . But just you look, two days later and it's a completely different story. He stops queening it up and the act fades away. (Louis 2018, 120)

What Clara misses here is that although Édouard has attempted to make himself "new" apart from his family, falling back into old habits in a hostile environment is not a sign that his new self is merely an affectation. These examples illustrate the way that the communicative scene gets cluttered with judgments and misunderstandings of Édouard prior to the experience he is trying to figure out. If Édouard were to attempt to engage in the kind of communicative endeavor he seeks, he would need first to clear up the detritus that has gathered around his pre-Reda self. In other words, if Édouard's project is to assign significance to and revise his practical identity in light of his experience with Reda through his communicative exchange with Clara, he would first have to engage the practically impossible task of making intelligible to Clara the self he seeks now to revise.

Clara's misunderstandings of Édouard's pre-Reda self do not merely accumulate around that self as static but drive competing interpretations of the attack itself. Consider the following example: Clara thinks that Reda had planned the attack beforehand and that certain traits of Édouard's personality caused him to miss what should have been detectable in Reda's intentions.[10] Clara says:

> They were lying under the covers, they were talking, and Édouard kept asking questions and the guy kept saying: Later, I'll tell you later. I can't understand why Édouard didn't start to suspect that something wasn't right. The guy was acting weird.
> And then she says yes, in the end she does know why I didn't suspect anything, it's because I latch onto people too quickly, I can latch on to anyone, it's been that way since I was little, and I haven't changed; but she wouldn't say this to my face, she wouldn't express this idea in front of me, because she knows I'd say I behaved that way, and still do, because of how alone I was, because I was always rejected by our family, and she says she doesn't want to hear that. Because it isn't true. (Louis 2018, 90–91)

Here, Clara constructs Édouard's pre-Reda self as hopelessly and inexplicably naïve rather than as lonely. The communicative scene once again gets stuck around misunderstandings of Édouard's pre-Reda character, such that if he were really to attempt to engage the task of considering the significance of that night to who he is now, he first would have to disentangle the misinterpretations brought to the scene. In cases like these, there is a sense in which the agent would have to "talk forever" to even get to the intended purpose of the communicative exchange.

---

[10] Édouard, however, does not think that Reda planned to attack him. He says, "(I don't believe it. Or maybe he planned to steal something, yes, he must have planned that part, but really I don't think Reda had any idea what would happen over the next few hours, over the rest of the night, not that this makes it any less violent or evil, but I think the whole thing happened in a stumbling, accidental, hesitating way, without any premeditation; I think he behaved the way that a person does who's trying to adapt to his immediate surroundings, from moment to moment; I think one improvisation led to the next, and that he was—I won't say as bewildered as I was, but that he, too, had lost his way, that he was at a loss. Once the situation changed, there was something improvisatory about his manner—I was there; I saw it—something that gave the entire scene an air of slapstick; there was even something funny—though of course I see this only in retrospect, when I look back—about his look of bewilderment; he kept looking embarrassed when he realized whatever it was he'd just done, it was as if he kept falling into a trap of his own making." He adds, "(Clara remarked the other day that none of these theories hold—he had a gun)" (Louis 2018, 91–92).

Édouard's attempts to communicate with the police and with Clara in order to develop the hermeneutical resources needed to make sense of his experience are frustrated because of how his interlocutors participate in the communicative exchange. The police instrumentalize his words for their own purposes in order to strengthen the racist bond between them and to confirm their heterosexual superiority and normalcy. The "resources" that arise from the exchange are useless to Édouard because his experience can matter in this context only insofar as it is instrumentally valuable for others. The exchange with Clara also frustrates Édouard's desire to engage with another in order to help him interpret his experience with Reda because Clara misinterprets his pre-Reda self and, furthermore, brings these misinterpretations into her understanding of Édouard during his experience with Reda. In both communicative encounters, his communicative need is unmet and he remains without the hermeneutical resources he needs to understand and revise his practical identity.

While the example from *History of Violence* focuses on a negative, traumatic experience, the same sorts of communicative failures often attend attempts to deepen the hermeneutical resources for understanding positive, joyous experiences in the lives of marginalized agents. In her novel *Next Year for Sure*, Zoey Leigh Peterson describes a character who is trying to make sense of her life and feelings but encounters communicative barriers that are similar in structure to those Édouard faces. Two characters, Kathryn and Chris, who have been and continue to be in a loving relationship, decide to open up their relationship, and Chris begins a relationship with Emily. Kathryn develops a close friendship with Emily and a friendship/relationship with Emily's roommate Moss. In one scene they are all together at a wedding:

> When their table is finally called to the buffet, Kathryn is left behind. She watches the three of them make their way through the line, choosing, discussing, considering.
>
> She has never felt this much love at a wedding.
>
> Kathryn is struck by a sudden urge to make vows. What promises could she make to these three people right now? All she can come up with is I will love you forever, which is hardly a promise at all. (Peterson 2017, 208–209)

While clearly her feelings for these people are significant to who she is, she is not yet able to express to herself how and why that is. She has available some generic hermeneutical resources, such as the concepts of an open relationship and of polyamorous love, yet she does not have sufficient resources for interpreting what participation in these kinds of relations means for her self-understanding and identity. When she seeks to gain further self-understanding through discussion with others, however, her experience is instrumentalized and her pre-experience self is misinterpreted. Other characters respond, as many often do when discussing poly relationships, with proclamations about their inability ever to engage in a poly relationship. In a discussion with one of the bridesmaids, the instrumentalization of this response is clear:

It must be so hard, Maura goes on. I could never do it.

Yes, you've said that, Kathryn says. It annoys Kathryn that this near stranger keeps volunteering her own inability like it is a point of pride. (Peterson 2017, 207–208)

This prideful proclamation of inability allows Maura to instrumentalize Kathryn's experience in the service of confirming her own monogamous normalcy and superiority.

Kathryn is also repeatedly judged as naïve, as lying to herself, as unfamiliar with the *true* nature of romantic love, as wronged (although opening up their relationship was her idea), and as in a bad relationship. Consider Kathryn's experience of being stuck in an afternoon of party games:

The questions are depressingly lascivious, and Kathryn can feel the women judging her whenever the topic touches on infidelity. Judged by Maura, who slept with their practicum supervisor when they were in grad school. Judged by Leslie, who talks about her husband like she doesn't even like him, and by Lorie, who just told them she has a pact with her husband about which five celebrities they're each allowed to sleep with, guilt-free. These are the women who will judge her? These are the people who look at her relationship with Chris—with Chris, who every Sunday folds Kathryn's clean underwear so that her favourite pair is on top and her least favourite pair on the bottom, who still mails Kathryn handwritten love letters from his office across town because she once said, years ago, that she missed the days of finding actual mail in the mailbox—these women will look at her relationship with Chris and be embarrassed for her? (Peterson 2017, 121–122)

While Kathryn wants to figure out her feelings about the new way she is arranging her life and the new relationships in it, she is judged by others as having flaws and personality traits coming into her new experiences that are entirely inaccurate. In these examples, although the experience to which Kathryn wishes to assign significance is a joyous one, the sorts of communicative failures Édouard faces repeat themselves here.

3.5. Concluding Thoughts

In *History of Violence*, we get an intimate portrait of a person trying to gain self-understanding so that he can engage in revising his diachronic practical identity after a traumatic experience. This need to revise ourselves in response to the things we do and our experiences in the world is a recurring part of being a self-governing agent. We do not and should not remain static and unresponsive to the experiences of our lives.

Édouard's particular story, however, draws attention to some important social aspects of our self-creative activities. First, where one finds oneself without the hermeneutical resources required to understand one's experiences, the relation between socially developed and supported hermeneutical resources, self-understanding, and self-definition, in short our ability to engage in the self-creative activities that make up one aspect of self-governance, is best understood as involving nested constitution. Without adequate interpretive resources, the materials needed to constitute self-understanding and self-definition are lacking and agency is stymied. Second, where the resources are unavailable for understanding some experience, the drive to communicate and potentially deepen the resources available should be understood as a communicative need rather than as merely one desire among others. A failure to have this need met opens an agent to harm to their ability to engage in self-governing activities. Finally, Édouard's experience in the two communicative contexts in which he attempts to fulfill this communicative need reveals two types of communicative failures that are common in the lives of members of marginalized groups. One may find oneself speaking into a context where one's interlocutors have the power to use what one says exclusively as a means to some extraneous purpose of their own or where, although one aims to revise one's practical identity by considering new experiences, one's pre–new experience self is systematically misinterpreted in itself and on the scene of the new experience. In these cases, it becomes practically impossible to consider the significance of the new experience to who one will be "now" because one gets stuck in the detritus that accumulates around misinterpretations of one's old identity.

4
Authenticity and Constitutively Relational Emotions

4.1. Introduction

In addition to competence conditions, which were the focus of the previous two chapters, many accounts of self-governance include some form of an authenticity condition. "Authenticity conditions specify what it means to be self-governing with respect to one's motivational structure, i.e., what it means for a choice, value, commitment, or reason to be one's own" (Mackenzie 2014, 31). The authenticity condition is meant to provide a mechanism for determining which features of the self, which values, traits, and desires, fall within the scope of successful self-governance.

Most accounts of the authenticity condition focus on an agent's assessment of a trait, on whether she maintains the relevant sort of pro-attitude toward her characteristics and motivations.[1] While theorists differ about what the necessary pro-attitude is (identification, endorsement, nonalienation), the presence or absence of the relevant pro-attitude determines whether or not a particular characteristic is authentic. Authentic characteristics are thought to issue from or be in line with an agent's true self, while inauthentic ones are considered in some way "foreign" to that self. One of the main tasks of the authenticity condition is to address how unwanted features of the self can diminish self-governance insofar as these features and the desires and actions motivated by these features do not fall within the scope of an agent's value system. Typical examples in the literature include what one does while in the grip of an unwanted drug addiction or under duress or subject to coercion.

---

[1] Meyers (2005), alternatively, articulates a skills-based view of authenticity. She argues that "the agentic skills of the self-as-social, as-relational, as-divided, and as-embodied, along with those of the self-as-unitary, belong among the reflective, deliberative, and volitional skills that comprise autonomy competency, for these agentic skills give rise to choices and actions that tap authentic attributes. In exercising these skills, one constitutes and enacts one's authentic self" (49).

In discussions of autonomy in general and self-governance and authenticity in particular, it is typically assumed that the self includes among its central features multiple constitutively relational characteristics. One's identity is not only shaped by multiple levels and types of relations but includes features that are constituted by our relations with others at both personal and institutional levels. The constitutively relational nature of these characteristics, however, are not often explicitly centered for analysis. In this chapter, I consider the relevance to autonomy of unwanted characteristics that have a particular constitutively relational structure, a structure that combines (a) something the agent deeply values with (b) unjust sociopolitical conditions that jointly constitute (c) an unwanted feature of the self.

I center for analysis two examples of constitutively relational emotions that are structured by politically supported or imposed forms of failed relationality. Following Lauren Berlant's attention to affect that arises "by the failure to resolve, repair, or achieve relation" (2014, 37), I center her account of loneliness (as longing for inaccessible love) and Sue Campbell's (1997) account of bitterness (as anger that gets insufficient uptake) for analysis. Loneliness and bitterness are common human emotions which are responsive to the social situations in which we find ourselves. As I will explain further in section 4.2 they both involve failures to achieve desired relations. These failures of relation, however, may arise from the ordinary contingencies of life that we all face as vulnerable humans living among others, or they may arise from unjust social and political practices that actively break or prevent relation. Loneliness that arises from the ordinary contingencies of life includes, for example, a parent's longing for a grown child who doesn't particularly care to keep in touch, a desire for a loving relationship with someone who does not return one's love, or the misfortune of living among others who do not share one's passions and interests. Bitterness as well may arise from the ordinary contingencies of life. One may grow bitter because one's repeated complaints are directed at those who have no interest in or obligation to give uptake to one's complaints. The clerk at the grocery store, for example, has no obligation to give uptake for one's anger at "the state of the world" or one's disapproval of the fashion choices of one's grandchildren or the peskiness of inconsiderate neighbors. These types of loneliness and bitterness, the types that arise from the ordinary contingencies of life, fall outside of the scope of my analysis because they do not arise from unjust sociopolitical conditions. Loneliness and bitterness, however, often arise not from the ordinary contingencies of life that we all face but from unjust sociopolitical practices. The parent who longs for connection with a grown child but lacks it not because the child has different values and priorities but because he is unjustly caught up in the prison industrial complex, is lonely for her child because of a corrupt and unjust political practice. The person who fails to achieve longed-for attachments in his community because those in his community are racist and believe that he has nothing of interest to offer others, is lonely because of unjust treatment. Similarly, bitterness can arise from unjust sociopolitical practices. Those with legitimate complaints about the treatment they receive in the world are often dismissed by those in power because the one expressing dissatisfaction is a woman or an immigrant or elderly. In these cases, people may become bitter because the social conditions in which they live construct them as people who do not deserve uptake and attention. It is these kinds of cases, cases where loneliness and bitterness are caused by unjust sociopolitical practices, which are relevant to my analysis.

I argue that the authenticity condition is not a useful way to discuss unwanted aspects of the self, such as loneliness and bitterness, which are not simply influenced by others and our past but are partially constituted by the unjust relations in which we stand. Instead, I argue that loneliness and bitterness, two constitutively relational characteristics that are constituted in part by something an agent deeply values and in part by a failure of desired relationality, provide examples for analysis that allow a focus on the interplay between one's values and one's social context. The diminishment of autonomy that arises from this interplay is best understood as arising from the way that constraints on self-determination also affect self-governance. While constraints on self-determination can affect the inner life of an agent *causally*, by decreasing motivation to act on one's values or when agents internalize the problematic norms reflected in the constraints they face, constraints on self-determination can also partially *constitute* elements of an agent's motivational system without getting purchase through the agent's sense of motivation or values.

4.2. Loneliness, Bitterness, and Their Sociopolitical Distribution

In addition to the various ways in which we are all thoroughly socialized beings who live our lives in particular relational contexts, central to one's self are numerous constitutively relational traits. Whether one is a sibling, a parent, a citizen, a neighbor, a student, or an employee is constituted by the relations in which we do or do not stand. While there are many types of constitutively relational characteristics of the self, I center for analysis two emotions, loneliness and bitterness, that are constituted, in part, by failures of relationality. These examples provide a useful focus because they are constitutively relational, arise from failures of relation, are negative, and bear a political analysis around questions of distribution. Questions of who gets or has or can afford to feel certain things bring together a focus on our deeply personal affective or emotional lives and the political conditions that govern the distribution of affect. Who gets to feel joy and security, who has to feel lonely or sad, who can afford to be hopeful or reckless, and who is allowed anger are partly a matter of contingent circumstance but also pervasively governed by sociopolitical conditions.

Lauren Berlant, in a tribute to Eve Sedgwick, identifies in Sedgwick's work attention to affective space that is constituted by failures of relation. She notes that "Eve developed many ways to gesture toward this space of inexistent relationality and one-sided attachment" (2014, 37).[2] Berlant's "focus is to elaborate these zones made by the failure to resolve, repair, or achieve relation" (37). I focus on two particular examples, loneliness and bitterness, that arise in this space of failed relations. While the contingencies of life make it the case that we are all vulnerable to being lonely or bitter, some endure an unequal distribution of these emotions precisely because oppressive social structures and practices interfere with and force one into positions of failed or broken relationality. My focus in this chapter is on the sorts of loneliness and bitterness that arise from unjust, oppressive, and exploitative social relations.

Berlant describes loneliness as "a kind of relation to a world whose only predictable is in the persistence of inaccessible love" (2014, 37). When one is lonely, one is oriented toward the world as desiring connection, but this connection is inaccessible; the relationality one desires is frustrated. The nature of the failed relation, of the lack of connection can take many forms. One may care deeply for particular people from whom one is *separated*. While everyone is to some extent vulnerable to such separations, cultural, legal, and economic systems mark members of some marginalized groups as vastly more vulnerable to such separations. For example, racist practices of mass incarceration use legal systems to keep apart those who care for each

---

[2] See, for example, Sedgwick (1993, 2000, 2003).

other.[3] Both those who are unjustly incarcerated and those who care for them are vulnerable to experiencing loneliness that arises not just from the contingencies of life but also from political and legal practices. Exploitative economic policies, work conditions, and practices keep the working poor continually laboring for bare subsistence, thus keeping these workers separate from family and friends.[4] Parents who must work eighty to one hundred hours a week to provide basic food and shelter for their families face loneliness for their children, romantic partners, and friends that those who enjoy less exploitative work conditions do not face.

Social conditions, moreover, don't just distribute loneliness by interrupting already formed connections; social barriers to making connection *isolate* people in systematic ways. Barriers in the physical environment render spaces of sociality inaccessible or inhospitable for people living with disabilities in unjust social contexts. Olsen explains that loneliness and stress "are the two main characteristics that accompany living with a disability in an inequitable society" and calls for "the removal of barriers which can prevent disabled people from getting involved in friendships, in social groups, and in social activities" (2018, 1160).[5] Heteronormative and homophobic social environments can keep queer people isolated from each other in many ways. Queer youths, for example, are particularly vulnerable to multiple types of isolation that keep them from forming relational attachments.[6] The queer teen whose parents forbid socialization with other queer people or who lives in a community without resources or opportunities to meet other queer youths is lonely due to socially enforced separation from others with whom they could potentially find understanding, camaraderie, and support.

---

[3] According to the NAACP's (n.d.) "Criminal Justice Fact Sheet," "[b]etween 1980 and 2015, the number of people incarcerated in America increased from roughly 500,000 to over 2.2 million." The racial disparity in practices of incarceration are clear: "In 2014, African Americans constituted 2.3 million, or 34%, of the total 6.8 million correctional population"; "African Americans are incarcerated at more than 5 times the rate of whites"; "The imprisonment rate for African American women is twice that of white women"; "Though African Americans and Hispanics make up approximately 32% of the US population, they comprised 56% of all incarcerated people in 2015." See also Nellis (2016).

[4] See, for example, Gilson (2011). For analysis of race and increased work hours, see Jones and Wilson (2017).

[5] See also MacDonald et al. (2018); McVilly et al. (2006).

[6] In their conceptual analysis of the kinds of isolation lesbian, gay, bisexual, and transgender youth face, Johnson and Amella (2014) identify "five socially constructed dimensions of isolation (social, emotional, cognitive, recognition that self is different, and identity concealment)" (524). Especially salient to the political distribution of loneliness for these youths are four subdimensions of social isolation: lack of social support, no contact with LGBT community, social withdrawal, and victimization (527–528).

A second example of an emotion that shares a constitutively relational structure with loneliness is bitterness. In *Interpreting the Personal*, Sue Campbell (1997) delineates the constitutively relational structure of some types of emotion by focusing on how the reception of expression structures the nature of what we feel. She argues "that what we feel can be individuated through expression to sympathetic interpreters and can be distorted or constricted in interpretive communities that are unsympathetic (165). One of the examples she uses for analysis is how anger is differentiated from bitterness. She assumes, for the sake of discussion, "that an expression categorized as bitterness begins its life at some point as intended anger" (167–168). The interpretive context in which the expression is made, however, can turn what was intended as anger into bitterness. Campbell, drawing on the work of McFall, argues that "[b]itterness seems to be a particular mode of expression—the recounting of incidents of injury—only in a certain context of interpretation—one in which people no longer care to listen. Both the mode of expression and the failure of uptake combine to form bitterness" (168).[7] Bitterness, then, arises at the conjunction of an expressive attempt about the wrongs one has suffered and an interpretive community that does not grant an agent uptake for her communicative endeavor.

Like loneliness, the distribution of bitterness bears a political analysis, and it is the instances that arise from unjust political practices that interest me here. Members of some social groups get sympathetic uptake when they recount the injuries they have suffered, while others do not. Campbell explains, "The accusation of bitterness implicitly acknowledges that a great many people have never been granted the social goods likely to lead to the luxury of cultivating sympathetic emotional lives. Bitterness does not always involve gender as a salient determinant of who is most likely to be accused. The angry disadvantaged of a society—visible minorities, aboriginals, the working class, the disabled, the ill, the divorced, and the old—are all targets of this critique" (1997, 167). Women, for example, who express anger about harassment are often dismissed as making too much of "innocent" encounters. The working-class man who was injured on the job due to unsafe working conditions is often dismissed as lazy or as "having a chip on his shoulder" when he expresses anger about the circumstances of his injury. Elderly people who experience pain are often dismissed or infantilized when they voice anger about inadequate pain management.

---

[7] See McFall (1991).

In analyzing loneliness and bitterness there are three components to consider: (a) the constituent of the trait supplied by the agent's orientation and values, (b) what is true of the social world in which the agent is embedded, and (c) what is constituted by (a) and (b) together. In the case of loneliness, (a) the agent is oriented as desiring connection, but (b) this connection is inaccessible, and together these (c) constitute loneliness. In the types of cases under consideration here, the inaccessibility of the desired connection is politically structured. Oppressive and marginalizing social structures and practices break or prevent connection through the systemic use of separation and isolation. In the case of bitterness, (a) the agent wants engagement with her accounts of the wrongs she has suffered, but (b) she gets no uptake in the context of expression, and these (c) constitute bitterness. As with loneliness, who is constituted as bitter rather than angry depends on who is constructed as appropriately dismissed and denied engagement.

4.3. Authenticity and Unwanted Characteristics

Characteristics of the self that are unwanted are typically thought to undermine self-governance when they fail to meet the conditions for authenticity. Generally, "[a]uthenticity conditions specify what it means to be self-governing with respect to one's motivational structure—that is, what it means for a choice, value, commitment, or reason to be one's own" (Mackenzie 2014, 31). The task of the authenticity condition is to demarcate when "foreign" influences, whether external or internal, interrupt self-governance. The decisions one makes while under external influences of coercion or threat are typically thought to be inauthentic and thus to be instances in which one is not self-governing. Some forms of internal influence are also typically taken as problematic for self-governance: "Apparent examples of internal forces that may threaten to usurp control from its rightful locus include addictions, obsessive-compulsive disorder, pathological gambling, kleptomania, and strong phobias. For those who prefer more-fanciful examples, the philosophical literature on autonomy also includes scenarios involving desires implanted through psychological conditioning, hypnosis, brainwashing, futuristic psychosurgery, and (that old favorite) supernatural intervention" (Noggle 2005, 87). In these cases, the agent "seems to be the victim whom they afflict rather than their author" (87).

Most accounts of the authenticity condition are articulated through an agent's pro-attitudes or lack of negative attitudes toward her characteristics and motivations. One of the main tasks of the authenticity condition is to address how "unwanted" features of the self, features toward which an agent does not have the correct pro-attitude, can diminish self-governance insofar as these features and the desires and actions motivated by these features do not fall within the scope of an agent's true value system.

Do unwanted, constitutively relational characteristics, like loneliness and bitterness, diminish self-governance? On the one hand, these characteristics are constituted, in part, by the agent's own values. On the other hand, external and unjust features of her social world combine with the agent's values and co-constitute characteristics that are unwanted by the agent. In this section, I argue that while loneliness and bitterness fail to meet the authenticity condition, they do not, for this reason, diminish self-governance.

As part of his historical view of autonomy, John Christman proposes an account of authenticity as nonalienation. Earlier, synchronic structural views, such as those developed by Frankfurt and Dworkin, proposed accounts that required much stronger pro-attitudes as the anchor for authenticity. Rather than requiring an agent to "identify with" or "endorse" her characteristics, Christman weakens the type of psychological attitude an agent must have toward her characteristics to accommodate the compatibility of some forms of ambivalence with authenticity.[8] He proposes that the sort of "self-acceptance

---

[8] Synchronic structural or hierarchical views of authenticity, as developed by Harry Frankfurt (1988) and Gerald Dworkin (1988), take authenticity to be a matter of coherence among the various levels of an agent's value system, where this coherence is signaled by pro-attitudes toward elements of that system, at a particular time. Synchronic hierarchical views face two main sorts of criticisms. First, synchronic structural accounts disallow as authentic a common feature of agency: ambiguity about some trait or desire. Mackenzie explains that the "criteria for coherence, such as identification, wholeheartedness, or endorsement, seem to rule out any kind of ambivalence or internal psychic conflict or fragmentation as inconsistant with self-governance" (2014, 31–32). Second, they seem unable to do the work they are meant to do (distinguish authentic from inauthentic desires) because of a regress problem. On these views, desire X is authentic if it is "approved" (where this notion is spelled out in various different ways, such as by being identified with or being endorsed) by a higher level desire. But on this account, there is nothing to guarantee the authenticity of the higher level desire, and thus it too needs to be authenticated and so on in an infinite regress. See Watson (1975). Mackenzie explains that "[r]elational autonomy theorists are critical of conceptions of self-governance, such as hierarchical or endorsement conceptions, which analyze authenticity in terms of structural features of an agent's will at the time of choice or action. The argument, in brief, is that synchronic accounts and criteria for authenticity that appeal to relations of internal coherence within the agent's will (e.g., identification, endorsement) fail to account for the historical processes of practical identity formation. In particular, they fail to account for the internalized effects of psychological oppression, that is, the way oppression shapes agents' practical identities and motivational structures, for example their preferences, values, and cares" (2014, 31). For an early articulation of this problem, see Friedman (1986). For Friedman's view of self-reflective affirmation as involving the

required for autonomy be read as non-alienation" because "[i]f to be autonomous required that we positively value each aspect of our motivational structure and conditions of action, only the supremely lucky and fulfilled among us would count as autonomous" (2009, 13).

Christman claims that "elements of the self may include factors whose appraisal leaves us ambivalent, so clearly not ideal from our point of view, but also which are not compulsions to which we are resistant" (2009, 143).[9] These kinds of ambivalences, he claims, can be compatible with authenticity; to accommodate this insight, Christman suggests "that the proper test for the acceptability of the characteristic in question is one where the person does not feel deeply *alienated* from it upon critical reflection" (143). On Christman's account, "[a]lienation is not simply lack of identification.... [I]t is a stronger reaction: it involves feeling constrained by the trait and wanting decidedly to *repudiate* it" (143). Moreover, "alienation is not simply a cognitive judgment, it is a combination of judgment and affective reaction. To be alienated is to experience negative affect, to feel repudiation and resistance" (143–144). On Christman's account, therefore, a characteristic will count as meeting the authenticity condition if the agent is not alienated from it on appropriate critical reflection.[10]

Despite the weakening of the conditions for self-acceptance from identification and endorsement to nonalienation, it will typically be the case that institutionally supported loneliness and bitterness will not pass the authenticity-as-nonalienation test. Loneliness and bitterness are constituted in part by the frustration of what one wants, and typically it will be the case that agents are alienated from and repudiate these characteristics. I do not, however, think that an agent's alienation from her loneliness or her bitterness is sufficient to undermine her self-governance. The constitutively relational structure of these traits allows for compatibility between self-governance and alienation from the trait.

Christman's authenticity-as-nonalienation view is an important improvement over identification or endorsement views because it can accommodate

---

whole self, see Friedman (2003, 4–5). For a discussion meant to deflate the significance of the infinite regress, see Noggle (2005).

[9] He offers the example of one's "attitude, say, toward one's children (and one's feelings for them)," which "may well be filled with ambiguities, complex conflicts, guilt, love, disappointment, and hope" (Christman 2009, 143).

[10] For Christman's account of what is needed for adequate critical reflection, see Christman (2009, 155–156).

the fact that we are often less than fully comfortable with and enthusiastic about some of our characteristics. His view allows the quite common experience of an ambivalent appraisal of a trait to be compatible with authenticity and self-governance. It accommodates, that is, the fact that we may have complicated responses to many aspects of our selves. The kind of ambivalence afforded self-governing agents by the nonalienation condition, however, differs from the kind of ambivalence that characterizes an agent's relation to constitutively relational qualities like loneliness and bitterness.

On Christman's account, there is some object, X (a characteristic, a value, a desire), in relation to which one may have an ambivalent appraisal as long as that appraisal falls short of alienation with respect to that object. For example, an agent may not enthusiastically embrace or endorse her attachment to her high school friends with whom she now shares little in common; she may be divided about the value of this attachment in her life; yet as long as she is not alienated from the value, she will meet the authenticity condition with respect to that value. The kind of ambivalence characteristic of the examples I have centered, however, is different. Suppose an agent is not ambivalent about her loneliness or bitterness but is in fact deeply alienated from these traits. On Christman's account, this alienation signals that these traits are inauthentic and thus that they diminish her self-governance.

I think that the dual constitutively relational nature of these characteristics should complicate our analysis. On one hand, one is not alienated from and may in fact deeply value the contribution one makes to the characteristic; one may deeply value a desire for love and connection or having a voice about the injuries one has endured. Yet one may be deeply alienated from the fact that the inaccessibility of love and connection constitutes one as lonely or that the refusal of one's audience to listen constitutes one as bitter. In these cases the ambivalence is different; one values one constitutive aspect of the trait but is deeply alienated from the trait itself.

Constitutively relational traits from which an agent is deeply alienated, which are inauthentic according to Christman's condition, remain compatible with self-governance because the agent values the contribution she makes to the characteristic. In these cases a person's motivational structure is complicated by the fact that what she contributes to the constitutively relational trait from which she is alienated is something she deeply values. She cares about her desire for connection or her ability to recount the wrongs she has suffered. While structural forces frustrate the fulfillment of the desires for connection or communicative understanding, she actively holds onto her values rather than being swayed to abandon them. In this sense, she does what a self-governing agent does: she keeps in place as part of her motivational structure things that matter deeply to her.

Second, although she is deeply alienated from her loneliness or her bitterness, when she acts from loneliness or bitterness she is acting as herself. Noggle explains that "to say that an impulse is not authentic is to say that it does not lie within that part of a person's psychology that must be in charge if she is to be genuinely autonomous (or that must be the source of her actions if they are to count as autonomous)" (2005, 88). In my view, when an agent acts from loneliness, her actions are motivated by a trait that is not authentic insofar as it does not meet the nonalienation condition, but such actions do not (necessarily) threaten her self-governance.[11] Consider, for example, an agent who is lonely because someone she cares deeply about has been unjustly incarcerated. Her loneliness motivates her to write letters to this person as a way to connect, to travel long distances at great inconvenience and expense to visit this person, and to get involved in political groups aimed at prison reform. While she is alienated from her loneliness and while she may deeply resent having to take the measures she chooses in order to try to strengthen the interrupted connection and cope with her loss, her self-governance is not diminished by the actions that are motivated by the trait from which she is alienated. The problem for her agency does not lie in the fact that she is acting from a trait that does not meet the authenticity condition. Authenticity as nonalienation is not necessary for self-governance.[12]

---

[11] Her self-governance may, of course, be undermined by the particular way that she acts depending on how those decisions fit with her other values. But the fact that she is motivated to act by a trait from which she is deeply alienated does not in itself undermine self-governance.

[12] For an alternative argument in support of the claim that authenticity is not necessary or sufficient for self-governance, see Oshana (2005). She argues that authenticity, understood as endorsement or nonalienation, is not necessary for self-governance. On Oshana's view, at least some of the traits that inform an agent's self-conception can be intractable and unwanted without undermining autonomy. She focuses on factors that are "acquired as the result of constitutive and circumstantial luck. These include certain idiosyncratic physical and mental abilities (strengths as well as afflictions), and the talents, temperament, gender, sex, ethnicity, and familial relationships that distinguish a person" (83). Oshana argues that authenticity is neither necessary nor sufficient for autonomy: "The concept of autonomy need not militate against viewing a person as autonomous even if she is alienated from an aspect of her self-conception. I need not be satisfied with, or feel an affinity with, every aspect of my self-conception if I am to be autonomous" (93). She centers, for analysis, race consciousness and claims that "[i]nsofar as ineliminable and scripted characteristics of a person's self-conception such as racial identity and race consciousness impugn autonomy, they do so for reasons quite different from threats to psychological authenticity" (91). The alternative reasons Oshana offers focus on practical control over one's life, on the degree to which one is able to be self-determining. Oshana usefully focuses on the power an agent actually has over her life. With respect to unwanted circumstantial necessities, she claims that "[a]utonomy requires that equilibrium of power be effected by the agent between herself and society. The possibility of effecting such equilibrium and the ease with which this is achieved depends largely on the energy that social navigation

4.4. Self-Determination and Self-Governance

Constitutively relational traits from which an agent is deeply alienated, like loneliness and bitterness, may be compatible with self-governance despite an agent's alienation from them. This is because the contribution the agent makes to the trait is something she deeply values, and this, I think, anchors her actions as her own even though she repudiates the relational traits themselves. Alienation from a trait does not necessarily signal a problem with an agent's motivations and values. Although I have argued that for these sorts of constitutively relational traits failure to meet the authenticity condition does not necessarily diminish self-governance, they nevertheless do matter to assessments of autonomy. Their constitutively relational structure reveals a constitutive interconnection between constraints on self-determination and diminishments of self-governance.

In her analysis of bitterness, Campbell notes "[t]hat the necessary public nature to expression gives others ways of controlling our affective lives" (1997, 163). If anger and bitterness are distinguished by the sort of response they receive in their interpretive context, then an agent's affective life is vulnerable to the conditions of that context. In my view, vulnerability to control by others, including institutions, social practices, and norms, is not confined to those emotions that rely on expressive context but arises more directly from the dependence that attends the constitutively relational. External circumstances, including the sociopolitical structures within which one lives, can control one's emotional life, for example, by keeping one separate from those one loves or by isolating one from others. Social practices that unjustly separate or isolate agents introduce a level of affective vulnerability to control that exceeds the vulnerability inherent in contingencies of life.

Sociopolitical circumstances that unjustly separate and isolate some agents or construct some agents as dismissible directly diminish those agents' ability to be self-determining. Self-determination "involves having the freedom and opportunities to make and enact choices of practical import to one's life, that is, choices about what to value, who to be, and what to do" (Mackenzie 2014, 17). In the cases of institutionally supported loneliness or bitterness, one's

---

requires. The invasive quality of racial scripting to self-management stems from the fact that racial scripting more often than not is disabling in practice" (92). In the case of the constitutively relational traits I examine, I too think constraints on self-determination are important and suggest an interplay between self-determination and self-governance in section 4.4. For accounts that move focus from authenticity to answerability for oneself, see Benson (2005a, 2005b); Westlund (2009). I discuss the answerability criterion in chapter 5.

autonomy is diminished not because one is alienated from these characteristics but because one's ability to be self-determining is constrained. The freedoms and opportunities others enjoy are not available to marginalized agents because institutional structures limit what they can do. In the case of institutionally supported loneliness, one may not have the freedom to be in the physical presence of those one loves because one, or someone one cares about, is incarcerated or continually working. One may not have the opportunity to form connections with others because of barriers in the social environment; one may, that is, be prevented from attending social events or important occasions. Likewise, one may not have the opportunity to express the wrongs one has suffered because others are socially supported in their ability to dismiss you. Unjust social practices that limit what one can do constrain an agent's ability to be self-determining. Unjust social conditions that separate and isolate and support dismissal diminish what an agent is free or able to do.

The problems for autonomy, however, are not confined to constraints on self-determination. Mackenzie notes that although self-determination and self-governance are distinct dimensions of autonomy, they are nevertheless "causally interdependent" (2014, 15). Centering constitutively relational characteristics like loneliness and bitterness reveals that in addition to a *causal* interplay between self-determination and self-governance, there is also, in these cases, a *constitutive* relation between the two axes. Constraints on self-determination do not only potentially influence factors relevant to self-governance; they partially constitute aspects of an agent's motivational system.

Constraints on an agent's ability to be self-determining may *causally* affect that agent's ability to be self-governing in at least three ways. In these sorts of cases, the main problem is that agents may *react* to these constraints in a way that raises suspicions about whether they are truly self-governing in their reactions. First, constraints on self-determination may lessen one's motivation to act on one's genuinely held values when, for example, those constraints place a heavy burden on one's actions. For example, limits on how easy or safe it is for an agent to navigate public space may undermine her motivation to do the things she values. Olsen (2018) recounts the enormous burden of resources that attends participating in many social activities for persons living with disabilities in an unjust environment. He says, "Many non-disabled friends seem to believe that all that is required to join them at clubs, events, or restaurants is to call ahead and let the location know that a disabled person is coming and, no matter the disability, the problem is sorted. In reality, it takes so much more than this. The location may be completely inaccessible, the environment may not be conducive to easy communication, and the number of people you may need to speak with may completely preclude your participation" (1162). Barriers in the physical and social environment and the amount of energy required to attempt participation in the social world in ways that reflect one's values can be so burdensome that they undercut one's motivation to act on one's values and desires.[13]

Second, constraints on one's freedoms and opportunities may be internalized as what one deserves or wants, and as a result, one may alter one's values and desires in ways that are commensurate with the constraints one faces.[14] For example, if an agent systematically faces dismissal when she attempts to communicate anger, such that she ends up constituted as bitter, she may come to believe that she is indeed making too much of herself or holding onto things she should get over, and she may cease her attempts to have a voice about the injustices she has endured. Social isolation may cause an agent to come to believe that she does not deserve or need connection with others, and she may then cease to desire it.

Third, constraints on self-determination may provoke unwanted and burdensome emotional reactions. For example, unfair distribution of freedoms and opportunities may cause one to become an angry person or a fearful person in response to one's social circumstances, despite wishing to live a

---

[13] Olsen provides the following example, which illustrates the unjust burden of effort and the attending diminishment of motivation to participate in the world as desired: "A personal example of this occurred when a deaf friend and I wanted to attend a concert together. I called the designated accessibility line. Here we were told that the only location where they could provide interpreting services was in a section which cost more than four times the cost of the tickets we had called to purchase, and that was inaccessible for wheelchairs. So, instead of spending that which we had budgeted for, we were being asked to spend much more, and to sit apart. After eight telephone calls, several emails, and my own explanation to the accessibility specialist about equality and disability rights, we were allowed to see the concert together and to pay the price for which we had budgeted. However, unlike those without disabilities, who can simply go online and snatch up discounted tickets for any event they wish to attend, it took me approximately six hours of work to attend one concert. I wish I could say this was a unique occurrence and was due to the unique situation of there being two of us with different disabilities. My lived experience tells me otherwise. A majority of the time the tickets are more expensive, they must be booked through a burdensome process well in advance, and the option to join friends at the last minute is non-existent. When the effort is given to participate, the time and stress of trying to make these arrangements work can often result in a net increase in stress for the disabled person. An event that was to be a place to meet new people, blow off steam, and simply relax with friends has now become work, arguments, and stress. The result is that the person often gives up on attending these and other types of social activities" (2018, 1162).

[14] Questions about when and why such adaptations of one's preferences matter to autonomy have been discussed extensively. See Khader (2011, 2012); Christman (2014a); Stoljar (2014); Mackenzie (2015).

more peaceful life. While these interrelations between self-determination and self-governance are important, the threats to self-governance lie primarily in the ways in which an agent reacts to the relevant constraints on self-determination.

Centering constitutively relational characteristics like loneliness and bitterness reveals that in addition to a *causal* interplay between self-determination and self-governance, there is also, in these cases, a *constitutive* relation between the two axes. Loneliness and bitterness are jointly constituted by (a) something the agent contributes and (b) a failed form of relationality. This partially constituting failed form of relationality, however, just *is* the constraint on self-determination. In the case of loneliness, a person desires connection with another or others, but the connection is broken by separation. To be unjustly forced to be separate by, for example, unjust economic conditions or unjust patterns of incarceration is both the constraint on self-determination (one does not enjoy the freedom and/or opportunity for togetherness that others enjoy) and the second constituting element of loneliness. Similarly in the case of loneliness that arises from isolation. A person desires connection with, for example, other queer youths but is unjustly socially isolated, so connections cannot be made or sustained. To be unjustly isolated is both the constraint on self-determination and a constituting aspect of loneliness. In the case of bitterness, an agent desires attention and uptake for expressions of the injuries she has endured, but she is constructed as dismissible and does not get uptake when she speaks. To be unjustly dismissed reveals a constraint on the opportunities one enjoys and is a constituting element of bitterness. In these cases the different kinds of failed relations (separation, isolation, dismissal) are both the constraint on self-determination and a constituting aspect of the agent's affective life.

This sort of interrelation between constraints on self-determination and features of the self relevant to self-governance is different from the kinds that function through decreasing motivation or causing one to alter one's values to match one's opportunities. Agents caught in external conditions that unjustly prevent relations they value face an increased level of vulnerability to external interferences in their agency. Oppressive social conditions that constrain an agent's self-determination can directly enter into an agent's motivational system by partially constituting aspects of her affective life. One need not internalize the problematic norms expressed in oppressive constraints on self-determination in order for those constraints to show up in one's internal life. An agent, that is, need not internalize the belief that separation from loved ones or social isolation is appropriate in order for these kinds of constraints to affect her inner life. While self-determination is thought to deal with the external and self-governance with the internal, these examples blur that divide insofar as the external constraint can structure deeply felt aspects of one's self in a way that isn't a reaction to the constraints but is constituted by these constraints. Unjust practices of separation, isolation, and dismissal constrain self-determination but are also foreign factors that narrow the scope of one's self-governance.

One way to understand that narrowing of scope is in terms of the nature of one's vulnerability to broken relations. Everyone is vulnerable to broken or one-sided relations. For some, this vulnerability is only a matter of the vulnerability we all face due to the contingencies of life. For example, in these cases one might be lonely either because one is thoroughly unpleasant to be around due to excessive criticalness or catastrophizing tendencies or because one has the misfortune of not meeting people with whom one shares sufficient interests. Those caught in institutional structures that break or prevent relations are doubly vulnerable, both to the contingencies of life and to sociopolitical interference. While the scope of everyone's control over their affective life is set by the vulnerabilities that attend the contingencies of life, this scope is further truncated for those who face interfering constraints on self-determination.

4.5. Concluding Thoughts

While alienation from a part of one's motivational system can signal a problematic failure to be self-governing in that respect, as is the concern in discussions of authenticity, it can also signal the intersection where one's own values combine with the constraints of one's social environment and create a particular sort of ambivalent agency. This ambivalent agency is not a matter of being divided or less than fully enthusiastic about some of one's characteristics but rather is produced at the intersection of a deeply held value, of a desire for relation, and one's sociopolitical context. In these cases, an agent may be deeply alienated from her feelings of loneliness or bitterness yet still be acting on her values when these traits motivate her behavior or structure her desires. The problems for her agency are not best located in her alienation from these traits but rather should be located, first, as constraints on her ability to be self-determining and, second, at the intersection of these constraints and the constitution of elements of her inner life. These constraints, which are forms of broken relationality (separation, isolation, dismissal), co-constitute elements of her motivational structure. While everyone is vulnerable to these forms of broken relationality, those who face separation, isolation, or dismissal due to unjust sociopolitical conditions are doubly vulnerable. The scope of their control over their affective lives is narrowed by these unjust interferences which do not just constrain what an agent can do but co-constitute elements of her motivational systems. In these cases, it is not that these agents *fail* to be self-governing but that the scope of the self-constructive component of self-governance is inappropriately narrowed compared with those who do not face the relevant constraints on self-determination.

5
Self-Authorization and Social Recognition

5.1. Introduction

Most theories of relational autonomy take social recognition to be crucial to an agent's ability to be autonomous. While theorists differ about the exact roles and functions social recognition plays in an autonomous life, one central site where social recognition is important is in discussions of self-authorization. In addition to self-determination and self-governance, several theorists also consider the relevance of self-authorization for autonomy.[1] Self-authorization "involves regarding oneself as having the *normative authority* to be self-determining and self-governing" (Mackenzie 2014, 35). More specifically, it involves "regarding oneself as authorized to exercise practical control over one's life, to determine one's own reasons for action, and to define one's values and identity-shaping practical commitments" (35). Regarding oneself as so authorized involves not only an internal, subjective evaluation of oneself but also a positioning of oneself in relation to others as answerable for oneself. Benson explains that self-authorizing agents "take ownership of their actions and wills by claiming authority to speak for their intentions and conduct" (2005b, 102).

This intersubjective aspect of self-authorization, wherein one claims authority to speak for oneself, is typically called the answerability or accountability condition. When discharging the answerability condition, one claims ownership of oneself by *actively* occupying a position of authority about oneself in social scenes where the giving of reasons and being responsive to the reasons of others is appropriate.[2] My concern, in this chapter, is with

---

[1] I follow Mackenzie in taking self-authorization to be its own axis of autonomy: "In the recent literature on social and relational autonomy, a number of theorists (myself included) have characterized what I am here calling self-authorization as a necessary condition on self-governance. I now think this is a mistake and that self-authorization is a separate axis or dimension of autonomy" (2014, 35). I think it is correct to treat self-governance and self-authorization as distinct axes of autonomy, rather than taking self-authorization as a condition for self-governance, because a constraint on self-authorization also may constitute a constraint on self-governance, but importantly, this is not always the case.

[2] The answerability or accountability condition is not identical to an agent's moral accountability; instead, it picks out an agent's active positioning of herself as the authoritative generator of her

Failed Relations. Rebekah Johnston, Oxford University Press. © Oxford University Press 2025.
DOI: 10.1093/oso/9780197795767.003.0006

how failures of appropriate social recognition affect self-authorization by undermining an agent's ability actively to occupy a position of authority as answerable for herself in relation to others. My main conclusion is that certain forms of social mal- and misrecognition preclude an agent's ability actively to occupy a position of authority with respect to herself in relation to others and that this undermines her position as answerable for herself.

There are two main perspectives that need to be considered when reflecting on the relationship between answerability and social recognition. The first concerns the perspective of the agent: what are the conditions under which she, from her subject position, is willing and qualified to answer for herself? The second concerns centering the social conditions in which claiming authority as answerable for oneself is possible.

Most accounts of the answerability condition focus on the first concern, on the internal requirements an agent must meet in order, from the perspective of her subjectivity, to be answerable. Accounts that approach the answerability condition from this perspective are typically weakly substantive positions. Agents who truly discharge the answerability condition don't simply answer for themselves but answer from a self-conception that includes self-reflexive or self-evaluative attitudes such as self-respect, self-trust, and self-esteem.[3] In the absence of these attitudes an agent may be either unmotivated to answer for herself or (at least temporarily) unqualified to answer for herself. Social recognition is significant to both.

Anderson and Honneth, for example, explain how insufficient social recognition can affect agents in ways that undermine their motivation to answer for themselves: "The importance of mutual recognition is often clearest in the breach. Consider, for example, practices and institutions that express attitudes of denigration and humiliation. They threaten individuals' own self-esteem by making it much harder (and, in limit cases, even impossible)

---

values, reasons, and actions. One may be morally accountable even in situations where one does not discharge the answerability condition. For example, one may deliberately excuse oneself of responsibility for a hurtful action on, for example, the grounds that one was merely joking, yet nevertheless remain morally responsible for the hurt caused. Alternatively, one may discharge the answerability condition without also meeting the conditions for moral responsibility. The answer one gives in discharging the answerability condition may in fact be exculpatory. For example, if called upon to "answer for" the fact that one rushed into traffic and caused an accident, one may discharge the answerability condition by claiming that one saw a child on the road and acted on one's value to aid those in danger.

[3] See, for example, Anderson and Honneth (2005), Benson (2005a, 2005b), Charles (2010), Govier (1993), and Mackenzie (2000, 2008).

to think of oneself as worthwhile. The resulting feelings of shame and worthlessness threaten one's sense that there is a point to one's undertakings. And without that sense of one's aspirations being worth pursuing, one's agency is hampered" (2005, 131). If one thinks of oneself as worthless and believes that one's aspirations and values lack worth, one will be unmotivated to claim authority over them by being answerable for them.

Discussions of answerability are concerned not only with cases where agents may lack motivation but also with cases where agents are unqualified to answer for themselves. Some cases are relatively straightforward. For example, a person who gives a family heirloom, say a necklace passed down for generations, to a stranger in a bar while extremely intoxicated is not, in that moment, adequately qualified to answer for that action. Some cases, however, are more complicated. Many feminist accounts, for example, focus on how the internalization of oppressive norms may shape agents in ways that trouble the claim that they are truly speaking for themselves. Mackenzie, for example, illustrates this concern with the case of Mrs. H:

> Mrs. H. does not have a sense of herself as having rights and does not reflect deeply on her practical identity. Mrs. H.'s drama is played out in an oncology ward where she has just had a leg amputated below the knee as a last resort treatment for aggressive bone cancer. Mrs. H. has lost her hair from chemotherapy and she is having to come to terms with the prospect of permanent disability, perhaps eventually death, although her doctors are fairly confident that her short to medium term prospects for survival are quite good. Her husband has recently left her because her disability would be burdensome and he finds her and her condition an embarrassment. Mrs. H.'s practical identity involves a conception of herself that is governed by the norms of traditional femininity that are taken as authoritative within her cultural community, and her husband's abandonment has left her feeling worthless as a person and without a reason to live. Mrs. H. informs her treatment team that she wants to die and that she wants no further treatment if the cancer spreads to other parts of her body. (Mackenzie 2008, 518)

Although Mrs. H tells the medical team what she wants, Mackenzie claims that her normative authority is compromised: "Mrs. H.'s decision to discontinue treatment does not seem to be underpinned by a strong sense of self-respect, self-trust or self-esteem," and the lack of these attitudes undermines her ability truly to answer for herself (2008, 525).[4] Weakly substantive views center the self-evaluative attitudes as significant to an agent's qualification to answer for herself, and these attitudes are directly tied to conditions in which one enjoys sufficient social recognition.

In section 5.2, I engage accounts of how insufficient social recognition can damage agents in ways significant to their ability to answer for or be accountable for themselves. I argue that a causal rather than a constitutively relational account of the importance of social recognition is both empirically more plausible and politically important. While I have been concerned throughout this book to center the insights afforded by considering the constitutively relational aspects of autonomy, in this case I argue that the constitutively relational account of the subjective perspective on answerability and the self-evaluative attitudes has the undesirable consequence of problematically truncating the scope of the claims marginalized agents can autonomously make. The causal account I defend leaves room for agents to be appropriately motivated and subjectively qualified to answer for themselves even from within contexts where they fail to receive appropriate social recognition.

In section 5.3, I turn to the second perspective on the relationship between social recognition and answerability. Specifically, social mal- and misrecognition may not damage an agent's motivation or qualifications to answer for herself, but they may practically de-authorize agents from actively occupying their rightful position as answerable. Specifically, I examine how some subtle forms of mal- and misrecognition displace and replace an agent's first-personal, experiential perspective from the sphere of answerability. Since it is this perspective that grounds her authority as answerable for herself, I argue that these practices withhold one of the constitutive conditions

---

[4] It is not entirely clear how Mrs. H's medical team should respond to reasons that are at the very least suspiciously informed by a lack of self-worth due to the internalization of oppressive norms of femininity. With respect to this case, Mackenzie asks, "How should Mrs. H's medical team respond to her expressed preference not to receive further treatment? Should this preference—based on the reasons she cites and at this point in her treatment—be taken as authoritative for Mrs. H.? Is the medical team obliged, out of respect for patient autonomy, to accede to her request? If the preference is not taken as authoritative, what options are open to the medical team consistent with respecting her autonomy?" (2008, 518). Mackenzie's own view is that "Mrs. H's autonomy is compromised, and so acceding to her request—for the reasons she cites and at this point in her treatment—would not in fact be consistent with respecting Mrs. H's autonomy. The appropriate response on the part of her medical team is to try to shift Mrs. H's perspective on her situation. But this approach need be neither paternalistic nor coercive" (519). How exactly Mrs. H's medical team should respond to Mrs. H's reasons is beyond the scope of my concern in this chapter; my point is merely to draw attention to accounts of how the internalization of oppressive norms can damage self-worth and trouble an agent's ability to speak for herself.

required for practical authority as answerable and thereby diminish an agent's ability to be self-authorizing. One of my aims in this chapter, therefore, is to shift the place of the constitutively relational in accounts of the answerability condition on self-authorization. Social mal- and misrecognition may leave an agent motivated and qualified to answer for herself but may constitute her as unanswerable because she, specifically the part of her that grounds her authority as answerable, is displaced from the scenes of answerability. She is, in these instances, subjectively motivated and qualified to answer for herself, but practically prevented by external constraints from doing so.

5.2. Social Recognition and Self-Evaluative Attitudes: The Causal versus the Constitutive Account

Self-authorization, "regarding oneself as having the *normative authority* to be self-determining and self-governing," is fundamentally grounded in appropriate forms of social recognition (Mackenzie 2014, 35). Mackenzie suggests that meeting the requirements of self-authorization involves meeting three conditions: the accountability or answerability condition, the self-evaluative attitudes condition, and the social recognition condition (35). These conditions are related; the answerability condition depends on the presence of the self-evaluative attitudes, and these, in turn, rely on appropriate forms of social recognition. But how should these dependencies be construed? While I think that treatments of answerability as essentially dialogical and of the self-evaluative attitudes as necessary for true answerability are correct, I argue against construing the relation between social recognition and the self-evaluative attitudes as constitutively relational.

First, the answerability condition requires "that the person regards herself as the kind of agent who can be held accountable and answerable to others for her reasons" (Mackenzie 2014, 35). Benson takes autonomy to be intimately related to an agent's ability and willingness to answer for herself; for Benson, "autonomy's normative substance resides in agents' attitudes toward their own authority to speak and answer for their decisions" (2005a, 25). Westlund, as well, centers an answerability criterion; on her account, autonomy relies "on the disposition to hold oneself answerable to external critical perspectives on one's action-guiding commitments" (2009, 28). Westlund helpfully clarifies that there are many ways in which one can exercise this disposition and that being disposed to hold oneself answerable does not require one to answer any and all external challenges.[5] This disposition, for Westlund, is dialogical or constitutively relational such that autonomy "requires an irreducibly dialogical form of reflectiveness and responsiveness to others" (28).

In many accounts, an agent's ability to meet the answerability condition relies on a second condition, the self-evaluative attitudes condition.[6] In order to be accountable, an agent needs to stand "in certain self-affective relations to herself, in particular relations of self-respect, self-trust, and self-esteem" (Mackenzie 2014, 35). These attitudes are significant both to an agent's motivation to move from a passive to an active stance with respect to her authority as answerable and to an agent's qualifications for being able to answer for herself.

Benson, for example, emphasizes the motivational aspect of the self-evaluative attitudes. He ties answerability to self-evaluative attitudes by emphasizing the active nature of taking ownership over what one does and values: "The key to comprehending the significance of reflexive, first-person attitudes for autonomy lies in the active quality of agential ownership. Persons cannot acquire ownership of what they do, in the sense that pertains to autonomy, simply by finding themselves passively in the position of owners. This sort of ownership is necessarily active; we can have it only by taking it" (2005b, 113). This active ownership relies on having a complex set of appropriate self-evaluative attitudes. On Benson's account, "[p]ersons can occupy the position of potential answerers only if they claim authority as answerers. In other words, agents do not acquire the authority to speak for what they do

---

[5] Westlund's dialogical answerability condition does not "rely on a willingness or ability to cite reasons on demand. It does, by definition, involve the adjudication of reasons in dialogue (of some form) with real or imagined others. But the form that both 'adjudication' and 'dialogue' may take is sufficiently broad that it does not commit the self-responsible agent to anything other than a formal condition that may be expressed in any number of substantive ways" (2009, 39). Westlund also clarifies that answerability does not require one to respond to any and every challenge. Challenges must be legitimate. While she does not "embark on the task of providing a set of necessary and sufficient conditions for legitimacy" (39), she proposes two important conditions: "First, a legitimate challenge must be situated in a way that makes relational sense of the intervention. That is, it must be situated in a relationship that gives context and content to the concern expressed by the critic" (39). Second, legitimate challenges must be context-sensitive: "a legitimate challenge must be context-sensitive with respect to the kind of response it invites and tolerates" (40).

[6] Although Westlund articulates and endorses an answerability condition, she departs from weakly substantive views by rejecting the claim that answerability relies on the self-evaluative attitudes. On her view, "we needn't encumber the autonomous agent with any particular conditions about herself. Answerability for oneself is a formal relation, constituted by a disposition to respond to normative pressures on one's commitments, not by any particular beliefs about or attitudes toward oneself. When one holds oneself answerable for a self-subordinating commitment, one's explicit values and beliefs about oneself may even manifest a lack of self-respect. What marks an agent out as self-answerable is how receptive she is to the critical perspectives of others" (2009, 37).

solely by virtue of satisfying requirements external to their self-regard. They must also treat themselves as warranting that position of authority, and the complex of attitudes this involves must contribute actively to their actually having authority as answerers" (114). The self-evaluative attitudes, on this account, motivate agents to move from passively going through their lives to taking ownership of what they do, what they value, and who they are.

The self-evaluative attitudes are also crucial to ensuring that an agent is qualified to answer for herself. Generally speaking, there is a normative requirement to respect the autonomy of others, to respect their capacity and right to answer for themselves. Mackenzie notes, "One compelling way of grounding this requirement is via the notion of epistemic humility. Since I do not know what it is like to be the other, or to be in her situation, I am obliged to recognize her normative authority over her decisions" (2008, 513). There are, however, cases that trouble this argument. Mackenzie explains that "the presumptive force of the epistemic argument seems less evident in certain difficult cases, for example, of addiction or mental illness, or even in some cases of oppressive social conditioning when the agent's practical identity does not seem to be fully her own" (513). Weakly substantive views of autonomy seek to ensure that an agent's practical identity is appropriately her own by introducing characteristics that must be true of the agent when she speaks for herself.

Mackenzie develops a weakly substantive account in which normative authority is grounded not just in an agent's practical identity but in a self-conception supported by the self-evaluative attitudes. She claims that "for an agent to have normative authority over her decisions and actions it is not sufficient that her reasons for action express her practical identity. In addition, she must also regard herself as the legitimate source of that authority—as able, and authorized, to speak for herself" (2008, 514). This "regard for herself" requires a self-conception that is supported by the self-evaluative attitudes. Mackenzie explains, "What underwrites this self-conception, as we have seen, are certain affective attitudes toward oneself—attitudes of self-respect, self-trust, and self-esteem" (527). This weakly substantive view ties authority to an agent's practical identity but includes the further claim that answerability requires also a self-conception that includes self-respect, self-trust, and self-esteem. It is these attitudes that ensure the self-conception expressed in speaking for oneself is truly one's own.

Self-authorization therefore involves meeting the answerability condition, and meeting this condition relies on the presence of self-evaluative attitudes like self-respect, self-trust, and self-esteem. The self-evaluative attitudes, moreover, rely on the social recognition condition. Mackenzie explains that "these self-evaluative attitudes are typically dependent on intersubjective social relations, that is, on whether a person is regarded as a respect-worthy, autonomous agent by others" (2014, 37).[7] Social relations of appropriate recognition are necessary for developing and sustaining the self-evaluative attitudes. There are, however, different ways to construe the relationships between the self-evaluative attitudes and social recognition.

On one account, the relation between social recognition and the self-evaluative attitudes is causal. As we go through life, we need to be recognized by others, valued, encouraged, and engaged, in order for us to develop and maintain self-respect, self-trust, and self-esteem. Benson's view on the relationship between the self-evaluative attitudes and social relations of recognition is ambiguous but seems to fit best with an interpretation that considers the relation to be a causal rather than a constitutive relation. For Benson, self-regard can be eroded in conditions of depersonalization and social invisibility. He says:

> Consider someone who, on the basis of race, has systematically been treated as socially invisible, as lacking the dignity of a person and eligibility to participate in distinctively personal forms of relationship, such as citizenship, friendship, or familial love. For example, imagine someone brought up within racialized practices that embody many of the attitudes that sustained chattel slavery and, later, Jim Crow in the United States. If this person has been depersonalized consistently enough, and if the personal attachments that might have given her a sense of her own dignity have continually been shattered or degraded, then she might come to internalize her social invisibility. She might regard herself as unfit for the kinds of relationship for which only persons are eligible, at least across many of the spheres of her social existence. (2005b, 111)

Benson's view importantly captures both how agents have multiple sources of support for the maintenance of a sense of dignity ("the personal attachments that might have given her a sense of her own dignity") and how

---

[7] Mackenzie acknowledges that "[i]t is always possible to find or think up examples of heroic persons who hold appropriate self-evaluating attitudes even in situations where they are despised and humiliated by others" (2014, 37). I think this observation is compatible with the causal account of the relation between social recognition and the self-evaluative attitudes developed below.

social invisibility and the shattering or degradation of alternative sources of recognition make one's regard for oneself vulnerable to inhospitable social relations.

On some views, however, the relationship between the self-evaluative attitudes and social recognition is not merely causally relational; it is constitutively relational. Anderson and Honneth propose a constitutively relational account of the connection between social recognition and the self-evaluative attitudes. On this view, the self-evaluative attitudes are not individually held traits, but are relational properties: "Self-trust, self-respect, and self-esteem are ... neither purely beliefs about oneself nor emotional states, but are emergent properties of a dynamic process in which individuals come to experience themselves as having a certain status, be it as an object of concern, a responsible agent, a valued contributor to shared projects, or what have you. One's relationship to oneself, then, is not a matter of a solitary ego reflecting on itself, but is the result of an ongoing intersubjective process, in which one's attitude toward oneself emerges in one's encounter with an other's attitude toward oneself" (2005, 131). On this account, the relationship between the self-evaluative attitudes condition and the social recognition condition is constitutively relational. The presence of appropriate relations of recognition partially constitutes the presence of self-respect, self-trust, and self-esteem such that agents do not enjoy the self-evaluative attitudes in contexts where social recognition is withheld. The emphasis in this framework is on the intersubjective character of the self-evaluative attitudes. They don't just emerge, causally, from relations of mutual recognition, but are constituted by those relations.[8]

I think there are both empirical and political/practical reasons to prefer the causally rather than the constitutively relational account of the relationship between the self-evaluative attitudes and the social recognition condition. First, an implication of the constitutively relational view is that if an agent is in a context where social recognition is withheld, then this agent cannot have the self-evaluative attitudes in that context precisely because social recognition is partly constitutive of these attitudes. It seems empirically false, however, to claim that agents cannot maintain self-respect, self-trust, and self-esteem in contexts of mal- or misrecognition.[9] In a recent article, Anderson reevaluates the constitutively relational recognitional view. He

[8] See also Stoljar and Voigt (2022).
[9] See also Johnston (2022).

says, "The first objection, then, is that the theory of recognition just sketched seems to be falsified by the existence of many people who are able to lead evidently autonomous lives despite being denigrated, neglected, abused, and disrespected" (2014, 142).

Second, in addition to being empirically inaccurate, the constitutively relational account problematically constricts the attribution of autonomy to marginalized agents. If the basic structure of the conditions self-authorizing agents must meet is correct, then answerability depends on the presence of the self-evaluative attitudes, which in turn depend on the social recognition condition. Members of marginalized groups are far more likely to experience failures of the recognition needed for the self-evaluative attitudes. As Mackenzie points out, "failures of recognition are quite typical in social relations involving domination or inequalities of power, authority, or social and economic status, especially when these are inflected by gender, race, ethnicity, or disability" (2014, 37).

On the constitutively relational view, agents' self-evaluative attitudes become too tied to the immediate context they are in, and this illegitimately truncates the scope of their autonomous agency. Specifically, in order to ensure that when an agent answers for herself she is appropriately positioned to represent her practical identity, theorists have suggested that she must have the self-evaluative attitudes of self-respect, self-trust, and self-esteem. If these attitudes are constitutively relational, then agents will not have them in contexts of social mal- or misrecognition, and thus they will be precluded from being answerable for themselves in these contexts.

Consider the following example that illustrates the problematic implications of the constitutively relational view. A woman working in an industry where women employees are ignored, denigrated, assigned the more menial tasks, and denied recognition as valuable employees does not enjoy recognition from her employers. She regularly faces disrespect and dismissal, and she does not receive adequate recognition for her work. If we adopt the view that the self-evaluative attitudes are constitutively relational, are intersubjectively constituted by relations of mutual recognition, this agent will not have the self-evaluative attitudes while interacting with her employers at work. But if the appropriate self-evaluative attitudes cannot be maintained in this context, then any protest or demands for change, any attempts she makes to answer for the value of her work will not count as autonomously made. For example, if her boss has no respect for her and continually takes credit for her ideas, any protest she makes against this treatment will count as nonautonomously made because her boss's lack of recognition for her work undermines his constitutive contribution to her self-evaluative attitudes, thus undermining her status as answerable for herself.

More generally, on the view that takes the relation between the self-evaluative attitudes and social recognition to be constitutively relational, marginalized agents will be unable autonomously to demand change in contexts where they do not receive social recognition. Even more troubling is that on the logic of the constitutively relational view, the reason they are not able autonomously to demand change is because they are lacking, internally, features that qualify them to make such demands. It is, however, precisely these contexts where demands for change are often most important. I think this undesirable consequence should make us wary of adopting the constitutively relational account and direct us instead toward a causally relational view. On the causally relational account, the self-evaluative attitudes are developed and maintained by and in our relations with each other. Experiences of oneself as loved, as valued, as respected are crucial to the attitudes one can develop and sustain toward oneself. More specifically, the social recognition provided by, for example, family, friends, political communities, representation in novels and media, and so on are causally necessary for the development and maintenance of self-respect, self-trust, and self-esteem. But, importantly, on the causal view, the relations of recognition we enjoy in one context may be sufficient to support the self-evaluative attitudes when one moves into contexts where one does not receive appropriate social recognition. On this view, agents retain the potential to be self-authorizing in conditions where social recognition is withheld. The causally relational account, in my view, is more adequate for respecting the authority marginalized agents have to speak for themselves in situations of mal- or misrecognition.

5.3. Practices of De-authorization

I have argued for a causal rather than a constitutive account of the relation between social recognition and the self-evaluative attitudes. While the self-evaluative attitudes will causally depend on recognitional support, they can survive in contexts where recognition is absent or withheld. If this is the case, then there will be contexts and situations where agents have the internal psychological infrastructure that positions them rightfully to be answerable for themselves despite the absence of relations of social recognition in those contexts. Social recognition, however, is relevant not only to self-authorization and answerability in terms of how it affects the self-evaluative attitudes. It is relevant also to one's practical ability effectively to answer for oneself. Mackenzie draws attention not only to how social recognition is important to the affective or self-evaluative attitudes but also to the fact that claims to normative authority are vulnerable when others do not recognize our authority. She claims that "our conception of ourselves as authorized to speak for ourselves and our claims to normative authority are dependent upon the recognition of others in the different spheres in which we make those claims: for example, the interpersonal sphere, in our work lives, as citizens, as persons who are both protected by and subject to the law, and so on. Because of this, the affective attitudes that underpin our self-conceptions and the effectiveness of our claims are also vulnerable to others' failures, or refusals, to grant us appropriate recognition" (2008, 527). While Mackenzie here continues to emphasize the relation between social recognition and the self-evaluative attitudes, she also shifts focus to the idea that our legitimate claims to authority as answerable for ourselves are vulnerable to failures by others to recognize that authority. Self-authorization, therefore, can be constrained not only when an agent does not regard herself as having the normative authority to be self-determining and self-governing but also when her authority is undermined by others' refusals to recognize that authority.

Anderson, as well, considers the ways in which intersubjective social recognition matters to an agent's ability successfully to vouch for herself. He suggests that "the normative pragmatics of vouching for one's self-trust, self-respect, and self-esteem" rely on "being recognized in response to one's asserting or claiming that one deserves to be recognized" (2014, 144). On his view, when one vouches for oneself, one is appealing to others for recognition. Specifically, "[i]n acting and choosing, we are asserting ourselves, vouching performatively not only for the appropriateness and intelligibility of our actions but also for our worth, our dignity, our place at the table. In vouching for myself—in claiming authority to speak—I am appealing to others for recognition. Succeeding at this is impossible for me to do alone" (144). Practices that withhold the social recognition needed for an agent to exercise her rightful status as answerable for herself can be expressed or performed in many ways. An agent can, for example, be assumed to lack the relevant self-evaluative attitudes such that what she says loses authority. In cases where there is a power imbalance, what one says when one vouches for oneself can be ignored, and in some cases the more powerful can intervene and interfere. Agents can also, for various reasons, be barred from the relevant scenes of answerability. One way in which agents are barred from these scenes is through the denial of what Anderson calls "participation affording competence ascriptions." Anderson argues that in some situations "essential elements of one's autonomy competence are dependent on attitudes of others in such a way that others' ascription of competence to us determines whether we get uptake in social practices" (146). On Anderson's view, "(1) some valuable modes of being autonomous are made possible within certain social practices and are strengthened by them in important ways, (2) these social practices require the mutual attribution of competence to one another, and (3) the unavoidably conditional character of these attributions means that aspiring participants are vulnerable to being legitimately (or illegitimately) excluded from participation on grounds of insufficient competence" (146). In addition to practices that exclude people from participation on the grounds of insufficient competence, I think there are further subtle ways in which social mal- and misrecognition function to exclude agents' authority as answerable for themselves. Specifically, I consider practices of social mal- and misrecognition that undermine authority by barring a person's first-personal experiential perspective or orientation from the sphere of answerability. In these cases, agents are not physically banned from the sphere of answerability, but their first-personal, experiential perspective, which grounds their authority as answerable, is displaced from that sphere. These practices preclude an agent's participation in practices of answerability by displacing the ground of her authority from the scenes of answerability. This reveals a constitutively relational aspect of the answerability condition.

Let me begin by considering some cases that show how certain forms of mal- and misrecognition undermine an agent's authority as answerable for herself. In order to see how the following cases undermine an agent's rightful status as answerable, consider the following typical ground of authority. Respect for autonomy is a central guiding principle in liberal democracies, and "to respect autonomy is to respect each person's interests in living her life in accordance with her own conception of the good" (Mackenzie 2008, 512). The demand to respect autonomy is often grounded in epistemic humility with regard to another's first-personal, practical identity. Because "outsiders" do not have access to another's experiential, first-personal practical identity, each person, and not others, has a right to claim authority over her life (513). In some cases, this normative authority can be undermined internally. Weakly substantive views, as discussed in section 5.2, secure this authority from an internal perspective by requiring the presence of the self-evaluative attitudes. An agent's authority to speak for herself, however, can also be undermined from an external perspective. What I examine here are two examples that illustrate a subtle yet pervasive way in which marginalized agents have their authority compromised by practices of mal- and misrecognition that exclude their first-personal practical identity from the spheres of reason giving. Since the ground of each agent's authority as answerable for herself is her first-personal experiential perspective, excluding that ground from "appearing" on the social scene functions as a refusal to grant the authority that is rightfully hers. These failures of the relevant forms of social recognition undermine an agent's autonomy by precluding her from participating in the answerability condition for self-authorization; they de-authorize her by relegating "the answerer" to a third-person perspective with respect to her own practical identity. Some practices of mal- or misrecognition have the effect of displacing agents' practical identity, understood as at least partially constituted by the perspectives of race, gender, and sexual orientation, from the public sphere and replacing those identities with a problematic alternative perspective. The following two examples illustrate the point.

First, consider the following story from Sara Ahmed's *Queer Phenomenology*:

> Another anecdote comes to mind here. I arrive home, park my car, and walk toward the front door. A neighbor calls out to me. I look up somewhat nervously because I have yet to establish "good relations" with the neighbors. I haven't lived in this place very long and the semipublic of the street does not yet feel easy. The neighbor mumbles some words, which I cannot hear, and then asks: "Is that your sister, or your husband?" I rush into the house without offering a response. The neighbor's utterance is quite extraordinary. There are two women, living together, a couple of people alone in a house. So what do you see?
>
> The first question reads the two women as sisters, as placed alongside each other along a horizontal line. By seeing the relationship as one of siblings rather than as a sexual relation, the question constructs the women as "alike," as being like sisters. In this way, the reading both avoids the possibility of lesbianism and also stands in for it, insofar as it repeats, but in a different form, the construction of lesbian couples as siblings....
>
> But the move from the first question to the second question, without any pause or without waiting for an answer, is really quite extraordinary. If not

sister, then husband. The second question rescues the speaker by positing the partner not as female.... The figure of "my husband" operates as a legitimate sexual other, "the other half," a sexual partner with a public face. Of course, I could be making my own assumptions in offering this reading. The question could have been a more playful one, in which "husband" was not necessarily a reference to "male"—that is, "the husband" could refer to the butch lover. The butch lover would be visible in this address only insofar as she "took the place" of the husband. Either way, the utterance rereads the oblique form of the lesbian couple, in the way that straightens that form such that it appears straight. (2006, 95–96)

Interpretive frames that "straighten" queers displace queerness from public spaces. While one may physically be in the space, a significant part of one's identity is excluded.

This exclusion, however, is not simply of an isolated trait but rather of an orientation toward and in the world. Ahmed explains that being oriented in a particular way toward the world more pervasively informs who one is and how one relates to other things.

Ahmed explains as follows: "I would say that being orientated in different ways matters precisely insofar as such orientations shape what bodies do: it is not that the 'object' causes desire, but that in desiring certain objects other things follow.... It does 'make a difference' for women to be sexually orientated toward women in a way that is not just about one's relation to an object of desire. In other words, the choice of one's object of desire makes a difference to other things that we do" (2006, 100–101). When one is "straightened," one's orientation in the world is displaced and replaced with an alternative orientation projected onto one by those doing the "straightening."

Second, in her discussion in *Visible Identities* of perceptual habits and visible difference, Linda Martín Alcoff writes, "In some cases, the perceptual habits are so strong and so unnoticed that visible difference is deployed in every encounter. In other situations, the deployment of visible difference can be dependent on the presence of other elements to become salient or all-determining" (2006, 192). To illustrate the latter sort of situation, Alcoff considers the example of an Asian American philosophy instructor teaching an introductory philosophy class in upstate New York:

White undergraduates walking into an introductory philosophy course in Upstate New York might not expect an Asian American instructor, but after an initial surprise the students appeared to feel at ease in the class as he (I'll call him "John") discussed Descartes and Leibniz and patiently explained to struggling undergraduates how to follow an argument in early modern texts. John himself then began to relax in the classroom, interacting without self-consciousness with a largely white class. His postural body image was at those moments normative, familiar, trustworthy. Despite the hierarchy between students and teacher, there seemed to be little or no racial distancing in their interactions. However, at a certain point in the semester, John introduced the subject of race into the course through an assigned reading on the cognitive dimensions of racism. This topic had a visceral effect on classroom dynamics. Previously open-faced students lowered their eyes and declined to participate in discussion. John felt a different texture of perception, as if he were being watched or observed from a distance. His previously felt normativity eroded, and with it his teaching confidence. It was not that before he had thought of himself as white, but that he had imagined and experienced himself as normative, accepted, recognized as an instructor capable of leading students toward greater understanding. Now he was reminded, forcibly, that his body image self was unstable and contingent, and that his racialized identity was uppermost in the minds of white students who suddenly developed a skeptical attitude toward his analysis and imparted it in a manner they had not been confident enough to develop before. (192)

Alcoff herself has experienced this change in positionality. She says:

I have experienced this scenario many times myself, if I raise the issue of race, cultural imperialism, the U.S. invasion of Panama, or sometimes issues of sexism in classes not self-selected for students interested in these topics, and colleagues of mine who are African American or Latino have described similar classroom experiences. Epistemic authority is shifted away from a professor of color when he or she addresses issues of race, away from women addressing issues of gender. Suddenly, white students lose their analytical docility and become vigilant critics of biased methodology. The visible identity of the teacher counteracts all claims of objectivity or earned authority as knower. Such an experience, as Eduardo Mendieta has suggested, is as if one finds oneself in the world ahead of oneself, the space one occupies as already occupied. One's lived self is effectively dislodged when an already outlined but very different self appears to be operating in the same exact location. (192–193)

Let me draw attention to three salient features from these examples. First, the agents in these two examples are not physically excluded from the potential scene of answerability. Second, although they are not physically excluded from the social realm, their identities, understood as their orientation in and toward the world, their first-personal, experiential perspectives, are excluded from the social realm. Third, they are attributed an alternative self. In Ahmed's case, the neighbor's "utterance rereads the oblique form of the lesbian couple, in a way that straightens that form such that it appears straight" (2006, 96). In Alcoff's examples, "[o]ne's lived self is effectively dislodged when an already outlined but very different self appears to be operating in the same exact location" (2006, 193). In my view, practices of social mal- and misrecognition that support these kinds of displacements and replacements undermine an agent's authority as answerable for herself.

How should we understand the way in which these practices undermine a person's ability to be self-authorizing? A person's authority as answerable for herself may be disrespected when what she says is simply disregarded by those who have the power to disregard her. In these sorts of instances, it is the content of what the agent says that is disregarded. Her first-personal experiential perspective is functioning in the sphere of answerability, but the content of what she says does not get uptake. For example, a person's audience may refuse to accept an agent's reasons as good reasons or as reasons at all.

In the examples from Ahmed and Alcoff, however, I think something else is going on. In these cases, it is not simply the content of what the agent says that is disregarded. The ground of her authority, her first-personal experiential orientation toward the world, is not only displaced from the scene of answerability but is replaced with a self that is projected onto her. This self, however, is not her first-personal perspective. Since the ground of her authority to answer for herself is her first-personal perspective, what is being displaced in these cases is her authority. Respecting another's autonomy involves granting her a first-personal status as an answerer. Epistemic humility, for example, requires that I grant another authority as answerable for herself precisely because I do not occupy her first-personal perspective (Mackenzie 2008, 513). One way, therefore, in which one can constrain another's autonomy is by undermining her right to that first-person perspective when answering for herself.

Let me clarify two points. First, there is a sense in which no one's first-personal, experiential identity is immediately accessible in scenes of answerability. This perspective, because it is first-personal, remains more or less opaque when one answers for oneself. The problem, in the examples under consideration, is not that these agents' first-personal experiential perspectives are opaque in the scene of answerability but that they are displaced from that scene. Opaqueness may make intelligibility in the scene of answerability difficult to achieve, but it does not, as displacement does, remove the ground of one's authority from the scene.

Second, this displacement does not simply remove the ground of one's authority from the scene of answerability and leave that space open. An open space retains the potential that an agent's first-personal experiential identity could show up in that space. In the examples under consideration, however, the displaced identity is replaced with an alternative figure, one that is attributed to the agent but is not in fact her own. This double movement of displacement and replacement puts the alternative, attributed self into the space of authority.

My suggestion, therefore, is that the sorts of social mal- and misrecognition captured in the above examples truncate an agent's authority by filling the space of that authority with a third-person, attributed perspective. By analogy to a physical replacement, it is as if I am excluded from the dinner party and the host chooses someone else to come in my place and speak for me. In order for me to regain my place of authority, I would need not only to show up and claim my chair at the table but also to eject my replacement from my spot.

These practices may have causal effects on an agent's motivation to attempt to answer for herself. The barriers may effectively silence her. Interestingly, Ahmed mentions that in response to the neighbor's "straightening question" ("Is that your sister, or your husband?") she rushed "into the house without offering a response" (2006, 95). She doesn't specify her reasons for doing so, but one effect such displacement and replacement may have is to silence the agent. In this way, these practices may reduce an agent's autonomy by undermining her motivation to be answerable for herself.

But even when these practices do not have this causal effect, in my view they function as constraints on autonomy. In the examples discussed above, an agent's authority as an answerer is undermined when a lack of social recognition displaces her first-personal perspective from the scene of answerability and replaces it with a self that does not have normative authority as answerer. This is a formal point about status—one can undermine a person's authority by excluding her from occupying the status position that grounds her right to be answerable. Consider, for example, the following scenario, which illustrates how an agent can be prevented from discharging the answerability condition due to practices that exclude an agent's first-personal experiential identity from actively occupying a position of authority in a scene of answerability. Theresa and Zahra are in a long-term romantic relationship with each other. Additionally, Zahra is also in a loving and romantic relationship with Jasmyn. While Theresa is not in a romantic or sexual relationship with Jasmyn, they consider each other family, are very close, and care deeply for each other. Theresa's family of origin, many of her friends, and many of her colleagues view the relationship between these three women through the lens of heterosexual monogamy; to use Ahmed's words, they "straighten their relationship." They construct Theresa as in a relationship of rivalry with Jasmyn, construct Zahra as unfaithful and insensitive to Theresa, construct Jasmyn as a threatening interloper, and construct Theresa as long-suffering in her willingness to "put up with" Zahra's romantic relationship with Jasmyn.

Unfortunately, after many years of living in this alternative family structure, Jasmyn dies in a car accident. Theresa is grief-stricken over the loss of this loved and valued member of her family. She decides to take time off work to allow herself a mourning period and to go away with Zahra to a cottage where the three of them spent many happy times together. Theresa's family and friends are concerned about her decisions and, out of concern, question her plan to take time off work and go away with Zahra. From Theresa's first-personal, experiential perspective, she is taking time to mourn an important loss in the company of Zahra, who also loved Jasmyn. Theresa's family and friends, however, have "straightened" the relationship and replaced Theresa's first-personal, experiential perspective with a third-personal, projected identity. Her first-personal perspective, as queer and polyamorous, is displaced and replaced with an alien third-person perspective, that of a monogamous, "cheated-on" spouse. No matter what Theresa actually says, these others interpret her as inappropriately taking time off work in order to care for her unfaithful partner, at her professional and emotional expense. In this scenario, Theresa's authority as answerable for her values and decisions is refused precisely because her first-personal, experiential identity is excluded and replaced with a projected identity on the scene of answerability. Specifically, her queer identity is replaced with a projected straightened version that wrongly takes her first-personal experiential perspective to be that of a long-suffering, disrespected, "cheated-on" spouse. Theresa is both motivated and qualified to answer for herself, yet she cannot do so in this scene because her authority is undermined by social mal- and misrecognition.[10]

---

[10] Theresa's family, friends, and co-workers withhold Theresa's position of authority with respect to her reasons due to their power to employ truncated and distorting epistemic resources that preclude Theresa's point of view from the scene of answerability. In chapter 2, I argued that unjust epistemic practices, specifically some instances of testimonial injustice, can narrow the scope of one's self-governance by truncating what one can intend. I considered the example of C, a Black man who

In my view, therefore, an agent's ability to be self-authorizing depends on her ability to meet the answerability condition. Meeting the answerability condition involves actively occupying, in scenes of answerability, a position of authority to speak for oneself. The ground of one's authority to speak for oneself in these encounters is a person's first-personal, experiential identity. Practices of displacement and replacement of that first-personal perspective with an alien, projected identity function to undermine an agent's ability to answer for herself by barring her from occupying a position of active authority in these scenes. In this way, a lack of appropriate social recognition of a person's first-personal, experiential identity constrains her autonomy by precluding her from discharging the answerability condition.

In section 5.2, I argued for a causally relational account of the connection between social recognition and the self-evaluative attitudes in part because to adopt a constitutively relational account inappropriately narrows the contexts in which marginalized agents can autonomously demand change. Here I have argued for a constitutively relational account of what it means actively to have authority and identified practices that diminish an agent's autonomy by precluding her from the relevant scenes of answerability. I do not find the latter account of the diminishment of autonomy troubling in the same way I find the former account troubling. The significant difference between the two types of cases is that on the constitutive account of the relation between social recognition and the self-evaluative attitudes, the reason agents are not able autonomously to demand change is because they are lacking, internally, features that qualify them to make such demands. On the constitutive view of the relation between social recognition of a person's first-personal experiential perspective in scenes of answerability and her

---

is stopped by the police while driving to work. The police officer refuses to extend epistemic credibility to C because of his racism. In my view, this case also functions to de-authorize C in the sphere of answerability. C's first-personal experiential perspective as a person driving to work is excluded from the scene of answerability and replaced with an alien perspective that takes C to be the kind of person who is engaged in criminal activity. This case is parallel to Theresa's case with respect to C's access to his rightful place of authority. It is not merely that the police officer challenges C by refusing to accept that "going to work" is a good reason for C to be driving. The officer, like Theresa's family, friends, and colleagues, exclude C's actual reasons for his actions from the scene of answerability and thereby truncate not only the scope of his self-governance but also his ability to discharge the answerability condition. The example of C and the example of Theresa differ, however, because the displacement of C's authority narrows the scope of what he can intend to do, while Theresa's self-governance is not affected negatively on the assumption that she retains the practical power to take time off work and do as she intends. Both, nevertheless, are constrained in their ability actively to occupy the position of authority required by the answerability condition. Comparing the cases of C and of Theresa illustrates a reason to take self-authorization and self-governance as distinct axes of autonomy; while constraints on self-authorization may also function as constraints on self-governance, as in C's case, they do not always do so, as in Theresa's case.

ability actively to have the authority to answer for herself, the truncation of autonomy is not attributable to an internal problem in the agent that disqualifies her from being answerable but instead is attributable to what others do to prevent her from occupying a position which she is both qualified to and has the right to occupy.

5.4. Concluding Thoughts

As many theorists have claimed, social recognition is crucial to autonomy and specifically to an agent's ability and status as answerable for her conduct, values, and identity. From an internal perspective, an agent's motivation and qualification to answer for herself relies on the presence of self-evaluative attitudes such as self-trust, self-esteem, and self-respect. I have argued for adopting a causal account of the relationship between the self-evaluative attitudes and social recognition on empirical and political grounds. Some agents do seem to maintain their self-evaluative attitudes in contexts where they do not receive social recognition. Moreover, the constitutively relational account unduly truncates the scope of the claims marginalized agents can autonomously make in situations where they do not receive adequate social recognition. The causal account better explains how multiple sources of social recognition can sustain an agent's self-evaluative attitudes and preserve her status as answerable as she moves into contexts where social recognition relevant to the self-evaluative attitudes is withheld.

Second, I have argued that from an external perspective, agents' authority as answerable for themselves is subject to constraint by some forms of social mal- and misrecognition. Specifically, an agent's first-personal, experiential perspective or orientation in the world is the ground of her claim to normative authority over her life. It is this perspective that makes her authoritative as answerable for herself. Practices of social mal- and misrecognition that displace her first-personal, experiential perspective from the scene of answerability and replace it with an alternative, projected, third-personal perspective is a refusal of her authority as answerable. While such an agent may retain the internal, psychological infrastructure, grounded in the self-evaluative attitudes, and thus remain qualified to answer for herself, she is constrained by others' de-authorizing practices in relation to her ability to occupy the position of authority that is rightfully hers to occupy.

Conclusion

This book has been about oppressive social conditions and personal autonomy. The concept of personal autonomy provides a nuanced vocabulary for identifying and describing what it means to live a life that is one's own. The multifaceted nature of the concept offers a useful mechanism for grouping together a wide variety of factors significant to determining the degree to which and the domains in which an agent's life is truly her own. These include, for example, questions about the freedoms and opportunities an agent has, considerations of her internal motivational structures, factors relevant to self-understanding and self-definition, and those relevant to the authority of her first-personal experiential perspective.

In its contemporary relational iterations, autonomy does not require escape from relations; it is a thoroughly social concept that provides important tools for analyzing the ways we are fundamentally always in relation. The concept of relational autonomy therefore provides an especially rich conceptual framework for analyzing the interplay between deeply personal aspects of the self and the sociopolitical relations that structure a person's context. The nuanced descriptions of the interplay between one's sociopolitical context and one's life that can be articulated by a focus on autonomy provide grounds for normative arguments for social change. Since liberal democracies explicitly aim to protect and promote autonomy, articulating the ways in which social conditions impede and constrain autonomy provides clear grounds for social critique and demands for sociopolitical change.

The central goal of my discussions and analyses has been to enrich philosophical treatments of relational autonomy by expanding the resources available for articulating the ways in which marginalizing and oppressive social conditions diminish autonomy. My focus has been on delineating the ways in which oppressive social conditions fail to provide the kinds of relations necessary for autonomy.

Living autonomously involves making one's life one's own. Following Mackenzie (2014), I structured the discussion of autonomy around three axes or perspectives that matter to autonomy: self-determination (chapter 1), self-governance (chapters 2–4), and self-authorization (chapter 5). All three axes are significant to assessing the ways in which and the degrees to which an agent's life is her own. An autonomous agent enjoys certain freedoms and opportunities in her social environment that support her ability to direct her life as she sees fit (self-determination). She actively participates in the construction of her practical identity, in who she is and what she values, and she regularly instantiates her values in her life through self-expressive activities (self-governance). Additionally, she actively occupies a position of authority as the source of her own reasons, values, and actions (self-authorization). All three axes map considerations that matter to an agent's ability to make her life her own, but they do not track degrees of success on a single scale. A person who enjoys multiple and robust freedoms and opportunities may, for example, fail to live up to her values or refuse to or be prevented from claiming authority as the source of reasons for how she does or does not make use of her freedoms and opportunities. Or an agent may fulfill the requirements of self-governance by actively participating in the construction of her diachronic practical identity and by regularly instantiating her values in her life yet may suffer a diminishment of her autonomy because her ability to be self-determining is constricted by a lack of appropriate freedoms and opportunities.

Making one's life one's own is significantly related to these different axes, and social relations are significant, in different ways, to all of them. In the existing literature there is a rich and nuanced philosophical vocabulary for describing the ways in which oppressive social conditions can have a causal effect on the autonomy of marginalized agents. Most of this work attends to questions and dilemmas that arise from considerations of socialization, especially gender socialization, and the internalization of oppressive norms. This focus lends itself to identifying **causally** relational connections between oppression and autonomy. These discussions provide valuable frameworks for articulating how oppressive social relations may causally affect an agent's values, motivational systems, and self-regarding attitudes in problematic ways. As I argued in chapter 1, most discussions of the relations between oppression and autonomy focus on and articulate the ways in which oppressive social conditions have damaging effects on agents.

My focus in this book has been to elaborate the undertheorized ways in which oppressive social circumstances are constitutively relevant to autonomy. The relevance of social relations to autonomy is not exhausted by their causal effects on agents. Social relations are also relevant to autonomy as constituting relations. In order to bring these types of relations into view, I have moved away from a central focus on socialization and the internalization of oppressive norms. Instead, I centered for analysis a different set of examples in order to emphasize, trace, and articulate some of the ways in which the constitutive relations needed for autonomy are absent, for marginalized agents, in social conditions of oppression. I have, for example, considered the implications for autonomy of living with those empowered to harass and engage in racial profiling, of experiences of epistemic injustice, of the political distribution of negative affect such as loneliness and bitterness, and of practices of displacing the first-personal, experiential perspectives of marginalized agents from the public sphere. These alternative considerations bring into focus the constitutively relational relevance of oppressive social circumstances to autonomy and, importantly, provide an interpretive lens that can accommodate the claim that an agent may not internalize oppressive norms and values in ways that damage her, yet may nevertheless find her autonomy constrained by oppressive social relations.

I take a focus on the constitutively relational to be centrally important for three reasons. First, it provides a fuller account of the autonomy vulnerabilities marginalized agents face. Second, the content of the broader account, insofar as it is constitutively relational, allows an analysis of autonomy vulnerability that directly identifies sociopolitical relations that constrain agents without the requirement that these agents internalize the values and norms expressed in these constraints. Marginalized agents sometimes resist the internalization of oppressive norms through participation in and support from alternative communities, but this burdensome resistance is not sufficient for addressing the constitutively relational constraints they face. It is not sufficient because the autonomy vulnerabilities they face are not reducible to nor solvable through the resistant psychological practices of individual agents. Third, since the solutions to the autonomy vulnerabilities marginalized agents face do not lie primarily in the cultivation of resistant psychological practices, a commitment to protecting and preserving autonomy requires directly addressing and changing sociopolitical contexts of dominance. As I outline in detail below, protecting and promoting autonomy will involve repairing the specific types of failed relations that constrain the autonomy of marginalized agents. Repairing these relations, moreover, will require alterations in marginalizing social structures and the dominating behaviors supported and allowed by these structures. The work that needs to be done to reduce the autonomy vulnerabilities of marginalized agents is work that focuses on altering the autonomy constraints inherent in dominating practices, not on the reactions of those who live with and in these constraints.

I have attempted to track and articulate some of these constraints by focusing, for the most part, on everyday, "ordinary" experiences of living with others in oppressive circumstances. What I have sought to bring into focus are some of the failed relations that matter to autonomy. These relational failures, in my view, constitute constraints on the autonomy of marginalized agents that exceed what can be captured in accounts that focus on the causal effects of oppressive social circumstances. There are four points about my analysis I want to emphasize.

First, living in oppressive and marginalizing social circumstances puts an enormous and unjust burden on marginalized agents with respect to their autonomy. Being regarded and treated, both institutionally and interpersonally, as inferior threatens agents' ability to make their lives their own. Causally relational accounts of the interplay between oppressive circumstances and autonomy provide valuable tools for articulating specific threats. What they focus on, however, is the ways in which agents react or respond to their social circumstances. For example, agents may react in autonomy-troubling ways by internalizing social messages of inferiority.

Some marginalized agents, however, manage to escape these autonomy-diminishing reactions or responses. Membership in communities where one is valued for oneself, treated with respect and dignity, and taken seriously as an agent can provide the social resources agents need to resist damage. Being required to engage in such resistant practices in order to secure aspects of one's autonomy is an unjust and heavy burden. Some agents, however, from within their particular communities of social support, are able to do so either globally or episodically or locally.

My central goal in this book has been to articulate the constraints on autonomy that remain due to oppressive social circumstances in cases where agents have successfully navigated the heavy and unjust burden of escaping the causal pressures on their autonomy. The set of constraints I've identified is not meant to be exhaustive but rather to trace some of the constraints that become clear through attention to the constitutively relational.

One of the things of value in tracing these constitutive constraints concerns the sorts of arguments for change one can make by centering concerns about autonomy. Accounts that trace the causal effects of oppression on autonomy can ground arguments for the claim that marginalized agents face a grossly unjust burden in achieving and maintaining autonomy and that this burden ought to be alleviated to the extent that autonomy is a social value worth promoting. Accounts that articulate the constitutive constraints on autonomy provide grounds for an additional kind of argument. Social relations that constitutively constrain autonomy are not just unfair and unjust burdens on autonomy, they are intractable barriers to autonomy. To the extent that we value autonomy, these social relations must change because they are not just burdens, they are incompatible with some aspect or aspects of autonomy.

Second, I want to emphasize the scope of the relevance of the constitutively relational to autonomy and draw attention to two significant points. First, while most accounts of autonomy, even when they leave room for the constitutively relational, are focused on the causal relations between oppression and autonomy, those few that do elaborate the significance of the constitutively relational tend not to focus on the self-governance axis but instead consider self-determination and self-authorization. Oshana (2006), for example, focuses on external social conditions that directly constrain self-determination. Others focus on self-authorization. Anderson and Honneth (2005) focus on the self-evaluative attitudes. Westlund (2009) focuses on a constitutively relational disposition to hold oneself answerable. In my treatment of the constitutively relational, I have discussed both self-determination and self-authorization, but much of my analysis concerns the self-governance axis of autonomy (chapters 2-4).

Assessments of self-governance focus on evaluating the inner lives of agents, their psychological profiles, motivational structures, values, commitments, and ways of defining their own identity. Given this focus, tracing the external world's causal effect on the inner lives of agents is both "natural" and valuable. Accounts that articulate how the external world causally affects the inner lives of agents in autonomy-diminishing ways are extremely valuable for tracing many of the barriers to autonomy marginalized agents face. In my view, however, self-governance is not immune to the direct constraints of the external world that characterize the relevance of the constitutively relational; self-governance is vulnerable not only to the causal effects of oppression but also to direct constraint.

Additionally, the scope of the relevance of the constitutively relational to autonomy concerns not only each specific axis but in some significant cases also the relationship between axes. Mackenzie takes the three axes of autonomy to be "distinct but causally interdependent" (2014, 7). I think this is correct, but there is also, in some cases, a constitutively relational interdependence between the different axes. For example, a lack of employment opportunities in one's chosen field fueled by implicit bias (a constraint on self-determination) may be internalized by an agent such that it has a causal effect on her ability to be self-governing or self-authorizing. She may, for example, falsely come to believe that she lacks skill and talent in her chosen field in a way that affects the accuracy of her self-understanding or diminishes her self-trust and self-esteem. While I don't mean to discount this kind of causal interplay, I have argued that a constraint on one axis of autonomy can directly constitute a constraint on another axis of autonomy. For example, as I argued in chapter 4, a focus on politically distributed negative emotions reveals a constitutive relation between a constraint on self-determination and aspects of an agent's emotional life.

Third, one of the things I find valuable about an approach to autonomy that centers the constitutively relational is that it traces constraints on autonomy without also encouraging paternalistic intervention or disrespecting the agency of marginalized agents. Many are rightly concerned that claims of diminished autonomy in marginalized agents will provide philosophical justifications for paternalistic interference in their lives (Christman 2004, 2014b; Holroyd 2009; Khader 2011, 2012, 2020). If it is respect for autonomy that prevents interference in another's life, then some worry that claims of diminished autonomy due to oppressive social conditions will end up justifying interference in the lives of marginalized agents. My goal in tracing the relational failures of oppressive social conditions was partially motivated by a desire to alleviate these worries by centering the ways in which oppressive social systems and dominantly situated individuals must change if we value autonomy. The failed relations I have articulated are not relations that can be repaired or remedied through adjustments to the psychological profiles, choices, or actions of marginalized agents. This is because the problems are not located in autonomy-diminishing reactions to oppression. The problems lie in the constraints of oppression. Accordingly, any interventions that can be justified in the name of supporting autonomy will not be paternalistic interventions in the lives of marginalized agents. Any interferences justified by my account will be interferences in oppressive social practices and the relations of dominance they support. One of my goals was to shift focus from what marginalized agents need to do to resist the internalization of oppression to the ways in which members of dominant groups and the institutions that support dominance need to change. Any interferences justified by my account will be directed at the removal or repair of relations that constrain the autonomy of marginalized agents.

Fourth, I want to emphasize that the failed relations that constrain the autonomy of marginalized agents come in multiple forms. Starting from the view that we all live our lives in relation, each chapter traces constraints on autonomy that arise from failures of the constituting relations needed for autonomy. The specific constraints I have identified focus on failures of relation caused by the pervasiveness of oppressive social conditions and the interpersonal dynamics they support. These failures of relation, of course, do not remove agents from relation but rather put them into problematic relations. I have identified and focused on five kinds of failed relationality that function as mechanisms that constrain autonomy. These kinds of failed relationality concern having the wrong relational status, the withholding or refusal of relation, relational absence, broken relations, and displacing relations.

C.1. The Wrong Relational Status

First, autonomy is constrained when the relational status between the dominant and the marginalized is such that the former are practically enabled to interfere in the lives of the latter. Social practices that enable a division of people into those who are "appropriately" subject to interference and those who are permitted to interfere structure social spaces according to a relation that is incompatible with autonomy for those in the former group. The relevant social practices that signal and perpetuate such a division include the fact that members of dominant groups are permitted to harass members of marginalized groups, to treat them as expendable, and to treat them as preemptively criminal. These practices and the relational status they reveal and perpetuate, as I argued in chapter 1, are incompatible with global self-determination. Global self-determination relies on the fulfillment of certain freedom conditions, one of which is freedom from living in social circumstances where members of dominant groups are empowered to interfere in one's life. A real and practical right to self-determination is conceptually incompatible with occupying a status that positions one as someone for whom interference is appropriate or tolerated.

This problematically constraining relational status, moreover, cannot be changed by altering the behaviors or psychological profiles of those who occupy the status position of those for whom interference is tolerated.

Appropriate social support for autonomy will require not only that members of dominant groups refrain from participating in these forms of interference but also that the social structures that make such interference practically permissible be dismantled and replaced with alternative relations.

C.2. Refusal of Relation

Second, autonomy can be constrained by relational failures that involve the withholding or refusal of relation. Members of marginalized groups often find themselves in social contexts structured by the withholding or refusal of ordinary relations. For example, marginalized agents are often refused the kinds of relations that would allow them, potentially, to be trusted, respected, believed, and understood. While these refusals of relation may be internalized and cause agents to come to believe that they are not trustworthy or deserving of respect, belief, and understanding, in chapter 2 I argued that these refusals of relation more directly constrain the scope of one's self-governance.

The competence condition on self-governance involves a self-expressive component. This component tracks the bridging of the gap between genuinely held values and the instantiation of those values in an agent's life. For example, an agent may value patience. The self-expressive component of self-governance tracks the degree to which she successfully exhibits patience in her life. Failure to exhibit patience, or any genuinely held value, signals a diminishment of an agent's self-governance because there is a gap between the value and the instantiation of that value in her life. Her autonomy is diminished because she fails to live up to her values.

Success at the self-expressive aspect of self-governance is typically considered using a standard competence condition. Does an agent effectively form intentions to instantiate X in her life? With respect to some values, this criterion works just fine. Specifically, it is sufficient to trace competence in instantiating values that do not depend on the active participation of others. It can, for example, usefully track the instantiation of values like kindness, patience, humor, and perseverance. This criterion, however, does not adequately trace the ways in which refusals of ordinary relations constrain self-expression. Some of the things we value are constitutively relational and depend on the active participation of others. For example, an agent who values earning respect or being believed needs the active participation of others if she is to instantiate these values in her life. One of the ways oppressive social circumstances manifest at the interpersonal level is through a pervasive and unjust withholding or refusal of ways of relating that make possible the instantiation of these types of constitutively relational traits. I have argued that social relations marked by the systematic and unjust withholding of the relations that allow the instantiation of ordinary relational traits in a life inappropriately truncate the scope of what an agent can intend and thereby unjustly truncate the scope of an agent's self-expressive activities.

Specifically, the scope of what an agent can intend is indexed to the scope of the terrain where her practical efforts potentially affect the outcome. One can, for example, intend to wake up early, intend to get in shape, and intend to be cheerful at odious social engagements. One cannot, however, intend to be immortal or intend to become a mermaid. The difference between what one can intend and what one cannot intend lies in whether or not one's practical efforts, what one does, are significant to the outcome. One can intend to wake up early because what one does the night before, whether or not one sets an alarm, for example, matters to whether one will wake up early. One cannot, however, intend to be immortal since immortality is not achievable through the practical efforts of human beings.

The standard competence condition for evaluating success at the self-expressive aspect of self-governance is insufficient because it starts from the position that intending to X is possible and evaluates whether a specific intention meets a standard of effectiveness. With respect to a number of ordinary relational properties that members of dominant groups take for granted, marginalized agents are precluded from occupying the assumed starting position where X is possible and effort matters.

Concretely, marginalized agents frequently find themselves in social contexts where others systematically and unjustly withhold their constituting parts of relational traits. One's sexist colleagues may relate to one in a way that precludes the possibility of earning respect; law enforcement officials may approach Black people from a stance of epistemic injustice that reveals testimonial injustice and precludes belief; others may refuse to employ the hermeneutical resources necessary to support understanding.

These refusals of relation constrain the self-expressive aspect of self-governance by truncating the scope of what an agent can intend. Relational traits, like being trusted, being respected, being believed, and being understood are, for the dominant, inside of the sphere where their practical efforts matter to whether they are trusted, respected, believed, or understood. It makes a difference whether they act in trustworthy ways or regularly disappoint people's legitimate expectations. It makes a difference whether they speak in an articulate or inarticulate manner in seeking understanding. It makes a difference whether they engage in or fail to engage in the sorts of activities that are the bases of earning respect.

Members of marginalized groups, however, face social situations where they are systematically and unjustly refused the relations that would make their practical efforts relevant to the outcome. When members of dominant groups unjustly and systematically refuse to relate to members of marginalized groups in ways that allow space for being trusted, respected, believed, and understood, it makes no difference what marginalized agents do or say. Their efforts are rendered useless.

In these sorts of cases, members of marginalized groups do not fail the self-expressive component of self-governance by failing to live up to their values. Instead, their ability to discharge it is preemptively prevented when and because of the ways in which members of dominant groups relate to them. In other words, they are prevented from living out their values. The communal competence condition articulates the barrier they face; it asks whether the community in which an agent is attempting to act is competent to support the *possibility* of the agent's bridging the gap between her autonomously held value and the instantiation of that value in her life. The community will count as competent when it does not withhold its constituting part of the desired relation due to systemic injustice. When the community fails to meet the communal competence condition, the self-expressive component of an agent's self-governance is inappropriately constrained; the scope of self-governance is narrowed in comparison to those who do not face these injustices.

The communal competence condition, importantly, directs attention away from what marginalized agents need to do differently to instantiate their values in their lives to the work members of dominant groups need to do to provide social contexts that don't unjustly constrict the scope of what members of marginalized groups can intend to do. The communal competence condition, that is, draws attention to the fact that in order to support autonomy members of dominant groups need to reorient themselves in the ways they interact with marginalized agents around issues of active participation.

C.3. Relational Absence

Third, autonomy may be constricted by relational absences. Marginalized agents often find themselves in social circumstances structured by the absence of the materials needed to constitute their own relations to themselves. In chapter 3, I focused on the self-creative aspect of self-governance. Autonomous agents not only enact their values in their lives but also participate in the creation of who they are. I argued that social relations can stymie self-understanding and self-definition when the epistemic resources from which self-understanding and self-definition are constituted are inadequate.

Self-governing agents actively participate in the construction of their diachronic practical identity. This participation relies on both self-understanding and self-definition and is not a one-time accomplishment. Self-governing agents engage in an ongoing process of self-revision that is sensitive to the ways in which new experiences matter to who one is. While self-understanding and self-definition are particular, they are not private. One's self-understanding is constituted by some subset of the hermeneutical resources available in one's social context.

When these resources are inadequate, as they often are for members of marginalized communities given that epistemic resources more frequently track the experiences of the dominant from their own perspective, agents are stymied in their ability to understand themselves due to the lack of resources from which self-understanding is constituted. This constraint on self-understanding will also constrain self-definition. Since self-definition relies, constitutively, on self-understanding, a constraint on the former will also be a constraint on the latter.

Agents in social environments that lack adequate epistemic resources for understanding their experiences face causal pressures on their autonomy. The absence of adequate epistemic resources may cause a decrease in an agent's motivation to engage in the work of self-understanding and self-definition. But even in cases where agents remain highly motivated to secure self-understanding and self-definition, their autonomy remains constrained. Their social context fails them because it contains a significant absence. Socially generated hermeneutical resources are the materials from which self-understanding and self-definition are constituted, and their absence constrains these activities despite continued motivation.

Agents whose self-understanding and self-definition are stymied by inadequate hermeneutical resources often experience a communicative need.

132 CONCLUSION

They need interactions with others that may potentially deepen the socially available resources for self-understanding. I argued that this communicative need is often left unfulfilled for members of marginalized groups and identified two specific ways in which communicative attempts are frequently thwarted by what others have the power to do with one's words. First, interlocutors in a communicative exchange commonly instrumentalize an agent's words for purposes extraneous to the communicator's needs. Second, interlocutors in communicative exchanges commonly mire an agent in misunderstandings of the self brought to the communicative scene. These practices frustrate attempts to generate additional, more adequate resources for self-understanding and self-definition and thereby contribute to maintaining the absence of adequate hermeneutical resources.

The nature of the failed relations with respect to hermeneutical resources involves both an absence and a use, but both kinds of failures require changes in the social context. First, social structures that sustain the paucity of appropriately nuanced epistemic resources need to change. The experiences and voices of marginalized agents need to be fully incorporated into the production of the hermeneutical resources available in the social context. For example, media representations of the lives of queer subjects, women, and racialized subjects need to do more than incorporate stock, palatable images that simply reproduce the understanding of what the dominant think is significant about living these identities. Second, individuals within social contexts, especially where a communicative need is being expressed, need to change how communicative attempts are received and used. Attempts to deepen the available hermeneutical resources through communicative interactions need to be received in a way that supports potential deepening. Using the words, stories, and concerns of marginalized people to reconfirm the "normalcy" of the dominant, and as a way for the dominant to bond with each other around that "normalcy," is one common mode of problematic reception that needs to change. Partners in communicative exchanges need to offer more than a practically useless (from the perspective of the one with the communicative need) instrumentalization of the communicative attempt. Additionally, members of dominant groups need to refrain from miring agents in fantasized but stubbornly entrenched ideas of who another is. When an agent expresses a communicative need for the purpose of developing resources to help her understand what some particular experience or set of experiences mean for *her identity*, gross misunderstanding of *her identity* frustrates the purpose of the exchange. She does not need resources to help her understand a fantasized and inaccurate version of herself; she needs resources to facilitate understanding of the self she in fact is.

C.4. Broken Relations

Fourth, autonomy may be constricted by broken relations. Members of marginalized groups face not only a constriction of epistemic resources needed to understand their own experiences, but also direct interference in their emotional lives. In chapter 4, I argued that constraints on self-determination can also constrain self-governance by directly constituting aspects of an agent's emotional life. My emphasis was on the ways in which social barriers are relevant to the inner lives of agents in cases where agents have not internalized those barriers as appropriate. Social structures that constrain self-determination through practices of isolation, separation, and dismissal need to be reconfigured not only because they constrain self-determination but also because they interact with an agent's values in ways that inappropriately constitute features of that agent's inner life.

Specifically, members of marginalized groups are vulnerable to unjust distributions of unwanted, constitutively relational, negative emotions. In chapter 4, I considered the significance to autonomy of unwanted, politically distributed emotions, such as loneliness and bitterness, which arise from the conjunction of something an agent values in combination with unjust political practices. An agent who values connection with others but faces unjust practices of isolation or separation is vulnerable to politically distributed loneliness. Likewise, an agent who values giving voice to the injustices she has suffered but faces unjust practices of dismissal is vulnerable to politically distributed bitterness. Emotions like loneliness and bitterness arise not just from the contingencies of life but also from unjust social practices that separate, isolate, or dismiss.

While it is common to address the significance of unwanted traits through the authenticity condition on self-governance, I argued instead that we should understand the threat to autonomy as involving an interplay between an agent's values and the self-determination axis of autonomy. Unjust social practices that separate, isolate, and dismiss are constraints on self-determination that directly constitute unwanted aspects of an agent's emotional profile. These unwanted emotions, although they will not pass an authenticity-as-nonalienation test, do not, due to this failure, signal the failure of an agent to be self-governing. When she acts from these unwanted traits, traits from which she is alienated, an agent nevertheless may be acting as herself in a way that secures self-governance.

The significance to an agent's autonomy is not best located in her alienation from these unwanted traits, but rather in the constraints on self-determination she faces and in the constriction of her control over her affective life. The constraints she faces are forms of broken relationality; she is unjustly separated, isolated, or dismissed. The forms of broken relationality, however, are not merely constraints on self-determination; they also constitute elements of her motivational system. Isolation and separation constitute her as lonely, and dismissal constitutes her as bitter. While everyone is vulnerable to isolation, separation, and dismissal due to the ordinary contingencies of life, those who are vulnerable to these broken relations due to unjust sociopolitical conditions which systematically constrain their self-determination are doubly vulnerable. Compared to agents who don't face these constraints on self-determination, the scope of their control over their affective lives is inappropriately narrowed. These agents don't fail to be self-governing, but the scope of their self-governance is constricted.

In these cases, the failed relations that constrict autonomy have failed because they are the wrong relations. Practices that systematically and unjustly trap agents in broken relations, relations that keep them separate and isolated or situate them as dismissible, constrict the scope of their control over their emotional lives. The persistent presence of these politically distributed broken relations in a life and the conditions that would remove them are not within the control of marginalized agents. The solution is not for marginalized agents to alter their behaviors, values, or psychological profiles, but for social systems that unjustly impose broken relations to change. More specifically, the solution to politically distributed loneliness is not for marginalized agents to alter their values such that they cease to care about or desire connection, but rather for unjust practices of separation and isolation to be changed. Similarly, the solution to politically distributed bitterness is not for marginalized agents to cease to care about voicing the injustices they have suffered but rather for practices of dismissal to change.

C.5. Displacing Relations

Fifth, autonomy may be constricted by displacing relations. In chapter 5, I considered the self-authorization axis of autonomy, which focuses on the normative authority an agent needs to make her life her own. Self-authorizing agents actively occupy a position of authority as the generators of their own values, reasons, and actions. Social recognition is crucial to an agent's ability to answer for herself and thus to occupy the relevant position of authority. A lack of appropriate forms of social recognition may significantly diminish an agent's self-evaluative attitudes or may displace the ground of an agent's authority from scenes of answerability.

With respect to the relation between social recognition and the self-evaluative attitudes, I defended a causal account. Self-evaluative attitudes such as self-respect, self-trust, and self-worth depend on social recognition for their development and maintenance. I argued, however, that a constitutive account of this dependence is too strong; agents can and often do maintain the relevant self-evaluative attitudes in social contexts of disrespect and denigration. While social recognition causally supports the self-evaluative attitudes, it does not constitute them.

With respect to the relation between social recognition and authority, however, I argued for a constitutively relational account. Certain forms of social mal- and misrecognition practically de-authorize agents by preventing them from occupying an active place of authority and thus constrain an agent's right to answer for herself. Specifically, some forms of social mal- and misrecognition function by displacing a person's first-personal, experiential perspective from contexts of answerability and replace it with a third-personal, projected perspective. Practices, for example, that employ a heterosexual and/or monogamous lens to interpret queer individuals involve a form of malrecognition that places a projected (and mistaken) third-personal perspective into the space of reason giving. Since it is an agent's first-personal, experiential perspective that grounds her authority as answerable, these forms of social mal- and misrecognition are direct constraints on an agent's ability to be self-authorizing.

These practices involve relations that fail to support the authority of marginalized agents. More specifically, they are failed relations because they are exclusionary; they exclude marginalized agents from actively occupying their rightful role of authority in scenes of answerability. Supporting autonomy therefore means that dominant agents need to cultivate relations with marginalized agents that do not fill the spaces of answerability with their own, projected fantasies such that the first-personal perspectives of marginalized agents are excluded from those spaces.

These multiple forms of failed relationality, the wrong relational status, the withholding or refusal of relation, relational absence, broken relations, and displacing relations, all constrain an agent's ability fully to make her life her own. They diminish her autonomy, not through damage but by functioning as inappropriate forms of constraint. Valuing the autonomy of members of marginalized groups who face these constraints therefore requires refiguring social conditions to eliminate these constraints. This refiguring will not involve paternalistic interferences in the lives of marginalized agents but rather will require the transformation of systems of oppression and the inadequate interpersonal relations they support.

References

Ahmed, Sara. 2006. *Queer Phenomenology: Orientations, Objects, Others*. Durham, NC: Duke University Press.

Alcoff, Linda Martín. 2006. *Visible Identities: Race, Gender, and the Self*. Oxford: Oxford University Press.

Anderson, Joel. 2014. "Autonomy and Vulnerability Entwined." In *Vulnerability: New Essays in Ethics and Feminist Philosophy*, edited by Catriona Mackenzie, Wendy Rogers, and Susan Dodds, 134–161. Oxford: Oxford University Press.

Anderson, Joel, and Axel Honneth. 2005. "Autonomy, Vulnerability, Recognition, and Justice." In *Autonomy and the Challenges to Liberalism: New Essays*, edited by John Christman and Joel Anderson, 127–149. Cambridge: Cambridge University Press.

Anscombe, G. E. M. 1958. "Modern Moral Philosophy." *Philosophy* 33: 1–19.

Aristotle. 1984. *Nicomachean Ethics*. In *The Complete Works of Aristotle*, vol. 2, edited by Jonathan Barnes, 1729–1867. Translated by W. D Ross. Revised by J. O. Urmson. Princeton, NJ: Princeton University Press.

Babbitt, Susan. 1993. "Feminism and Objective Interests: The Role of Transformative Experiences in Rational Deliberation." In *Feminist Epistemologies*, edited by Linda Alcoff and Elizabeth Potter, 245–264. New York: Routledge.

Benson, Paul. 1991. "Autonomy and Oppressive Socialization." *Social Theory and Practice* 17(3): 385–408.

Benson, Paul. 1994. "Free Agency and Self-Worth." *Journal of Philosophy* 91: 650–668.

Benson, Paul. 2000. "Feeling Crazy: Self-Worth and the Social Character of Responsibility." In *Relational Autonomy: Feminist Perspectives on Autonomy, Agency, and the Social Self*, edited by Catriona Mackenzie and Natalie Stoljar, 72–93. New York: Oxford University Press.

Benson, Paul. 2005a. "Feminist Intuitions and the Normative Substance of Autonomy." In *Personal Autonomy: New Essays on Personal Autonomy and Its Role in Contemporary Moral Philosophy*, edited by James Stacey Taylor, 124–142. Cambridge: Cambridge University Press.

Benson, Paul. 2005b. "Taking Ownership: Authority and Voice in Autonomous Agency." In *Autonomy and the Challenges to Liberalism: New Essays*, edited by John Christman and Joel Anderson, 101–126. Cambridge: Cambridge University Press.

Berenstain, Nora. 2016. "Epistemic Exploitation." *Ergo* 3(22): 569–590.

Berlant, Lauren, and Lee Edelman. 2014. *Sex, or the Unbearable*. Durham, NC: Duke University Press.

Berofsky, Bernard. 1995. *Liberation from Self: A Theory of Personal Autonomy*. New York: Routledge and Kegan Paul.

Brison, Susan J. 2002. *Aftermath: Violence and the Remaking of a Self*. Princeton, NJ: Princeton University Press.

Campbell, Sue. 1997. *Interpreting the Personal: Expression and the Formation of Feelings*. Ithaca, NY: Cornell University Press.

Charles, Sonya. 2010. "How Should Feminist Autonomy Theorists Respond to the Problem of Internalized Oppression?" *Social Theory and Practice* 36(3): 409–428.

Chemaly, Soraya. 2018. *Rage Becomes Her: The Power of Women's Anger*. New York: Atria Books.

Christman, John. 2004. "Relational Autonomy, Liberal Individualism, and the Social Constitution of Selves." *Philosophical Studies* 117: 143–164.

REFERENCES

Christman, John. 2009. *The Politics of Persons: Individual Autonomy and Socio-Historical Selves.* Cambridge: Cambridge University Press.

Christman, John. 2014a. "Coping or Oppression: Autonomy and Adaptation to Circumstance." In *Autonomy, Oppression, and Gender*, edited by Andrea Veltman and Mark Piper, 201–226. New York: Oxford University Press.

Christman, John. 2014b. "Relational Autonomy and the Social Dynamics of Paternalism." *Ethical Theory and Moral Practice* 17: 369–382.

Cooper, Brittney. 2018. *Eloquent Rage: A Black Feminist Discovers Her Superpower.* New York: St. Martin's Press.

Dotson, Kristie. 2011. "Tracking Epistemic Violence, Tracking Practices of Silencing." *Hypatia* 26(2): 236–257.

Dotson, Kristie. 2012. "A Cautionary Tale: On Limiting Epistemic Oppression." *Frontiers* 33(1): 24–47.

Dworkin, Gerald. 1988. *The Theory and Practice of Autonomy.* New York: Cambridge University Press.

Feinburg, Joel. 1973. *Social Philosophy.* Englewood Cliffs, NJ: Prentice-Hall.

Frankfurt, Harry. 1988. *The Importance of What We Care About.* Cambridge: Cambridge University Press.

Fricker, Miranda. 2007. *Epistemic Injustice: Power and the Ethics of Knowing.* Oxford: Oxford University Press.

Friedman, Marilyn A. 1986. "Autonomy and the Split-Level Self." *Southern Journal of Philosophy* 24(1): 19–35.

Friedman, Marilyn A. 2003. *Autonomy, Gender, Politics.* New York: Oxford University Press.

Gilson, Dave. 2011. "Speedup Americans Working Harder Charts." *Mother Jones*, May. https://www.motherjones.com/politics/2011/05/speedup-americans-working-harder-charts/.

Govier, Trudy. 1993. "Self-Trust, Autonomy, and Self-Esteem." *Hypatia* 8(1): 99–120.

Hoffman, Eva. 1989. *Lost in Translation.* New York: Dutton.

Holroyd, Jules. 2009. "Relational Autonomy and Paternalistic Intervention." *Res Publica* 15: 321–336.

Johnson, Michael, and Elaine Amella. 2014. "Isolation of Lesbian, Gay, Bisexual and Transgender Youth: A Dimensional Concept Analysis." *Advanced Journal of Nursing* 70(3): 523–532.

Johnston, Rebekah. 2017. "Personal Autonomy, Social Identity, and Oppressive Social Contexts." *Hypatia* 32(2): 312–328.

Johnston, Rebekah. 2022. "Autonomy, Relational Egalitarianism, and Indignation." In *Relational Autonomy and Relational Equality*, edited by Natalie Stoljar and Kristin Voigt, 125–144. New York: Routledge.

Jones, Janelle, and Valerie Wilson. 2017. "Low-Wage African American Workers Have Increased Annual Work Hours Most since 1979." Economic Policy Institute. https://www.epi.org/blog/low-wage-african-american-workers-have-increased-annual-work-hours-most-since-1979/.

Khader, Serene J. 2011. *Adaptive Preferences and Women's Empowerment.* New York: Oxford University Press.

Khader, Serene J. 2012. "Must Theorizing about Adaptive Preferences Deny Women's Agency?" *Journal of Applied Philosophy* 29(4): 302–317.

Khader, Serene J. 2020. "The Feminist Case against Relational Autonomy." *Journal of Moral Philosophy* 17(5): 499–526.

Killmister, Suzy. 2015. "Autonomy under Oppression: Tensions, Trade-Offs, and Resistance." In *Personal Autonomy and Social Oppression: Philosophical Perspectives*, edited by Marina A. L. Oshana, 161–180. New York: Routledge.

Louis, Édouard. 2017. *The End of Eddy.* Translated by Michael Lucey. New York: Picador, Farrar, Straus, and Giroux.

Louis, Édouard. 2018. *History of Violence*. Translated by Lorin Stein. New York: Farrar, Straus and Giroux.

Lugones, Maria, and Elizabeth Spelman. 1986. "Have We Got a Theory for You! Feminist Theory, Cultural Imperialism and the Demand for 'the Woman's Voice.'" In Women and Values, edited by Marilyn Pearsall, 19–31. Belmont, CA: Wadsworth.

MacDonald, Stephen J., Lesley Deacon, Jackie Nixon, Abisope Akintola, Anna Gillingham, Jacqueline Kent, Gillian Ellis, Debbie Mathews, Abolaji Ismail, Sylvia Sullivan, Samouka Dore, and Liz Highmore. 2018. "'The Invisible Enemy': Disability, Loneliness, and Isolation." *Disability & Society* 33(7): 1138–1159.

Mackenzie, Catriona. 2000. "Imagining Oneself Otherwise." In *Relational Autonomy: Feminist Perspectives on Autonomy, Agency, and the Social Self*, edited by Catriona Mackenzie and Natalie Stoljar, 124–150. New York: Oxford University Press.

Mackenzie, Catriona. 2002. "Critical Reflection, Self-Knowledge, and the Emotions." *Philosophical Explorations* 5(2): 186–206.

Mackenzie, Catriona. 2008. "Relational Autonomy, Normative Authority, and Perfectionism." *Journal of Social Philosophy* 39(4): 512–533.

Mackenzie, Catriona. 2014. "Three Dimensions of Autonomy: A Relational Analysis." In *Autonomy, Oppression, and Gender*, edited by Andrea Veltman and Mark Piper, 15–41. New York: Oxford University Press.

Mackenzie, Catriona. 2015. "Responding to the Agency Dilemma: Autonomy, Adaptive Preferences, and Internalized Oppression." In *Personal Autonomy and Social Oppression: Philosophical Perspectives*, edited by Marina A. L. Oshana, 48–67. New York: Routledge.

Mackenzie, Catriona, and Natalie Stoljar, eds. 2000. *Relational Autonomy: Feminist Perspectives on Autonomy, Agency, and the Social Self*. New York: Oxford University Press.

McFall, Lynn. 1991. "What's Wrong with Bitterness?" In *Feminist Ethics*, edited by Claudia Card, 146–160. Lawrence: University of Kansas Press.

McVilly, Keith R., Robert J. Stancliffe, Trevor R. Parmenter, and Rosanne M. Burton-Smith. 2006. "'I Get By with a Little Help from My Friends': Adults with Intellectual Disability Discuss Loneliness." *Journal of Applied Research in Intellectual Disabilities* 19: 191–203.

Medina, José. 2013. *The Epistemology of Resistance*. Oxford: Oxford University Press.

Medina, José. 2017. "Epistemic Injustice and Epistemologies of Ignorance." In *The Routledge Companion to the Philosophy of Race*, edited by Paul Taylor, Linda Martín Alcoff, and Luvell Anderson, 247–260. London: Routledge.

Meyers, Diana Tietjens. 1989. *Self, Society, and Personal Choice*. New York: Columbia University Press.

Meyers, Diana Tietjens. 2002. *Gender in the Mirror: Cultural Imagery and Women's Agency*. Oxford: Oxford University Press.

Meyers, Diana Tietjens. 2014. "The Feminist Debate over Values in Autonomy Theory." In *Autonomy, Oppression, and Gender*, edited by Andrea Veltman and Mark Piper, 114–140. New York: Oxford University Press.

NAACP. n.d. "Criminal Justice Fact Sheet." Accessed June 19, 2019. https://www.naacp.org/criminal-justice-fact-sheet/.

Nellis, Ashley. 2021. "The Color of Justice: Racial and Ethnic Disparity in State Prisons." Sentencing Project. https:www.sentencingproject.org/publications/color-of-justice-racial-and-ethnic-disparity-in-state-prisons/.

Noggle, Robert. 2005. "Autonomy and the Paradox of Self-Creation: Infinite Regresses, Finite Selves, and the Limits of Authenticity." In *Personal Autonomy: New Essays on Personal Autonomy and Its Role in Contemporary Moral Philosophy*, edited by James Stacey Taylor, 87–108. Cambridge: Cambridge University Press.

Olsen, Jason. 2018. "Socially Disabled: The Fight Disabled People Face against Loneliness and Stress." *Disability & Society* 33(7): 1160–1164.

Oshana, Marina. 2005. "Autonomy and Self-Identity." In *Autonomy and the Challenges to Liberalism: New Essays*, edited by John Christman and Joel Anderson, 77–97. Cambridge: Cambridge University Press.

Oshana, Marina. 2006. *Personal Autonomy in Society*. Hampshire: Ashgate.

Peet, Andrew. 2017. "Epistemic Injustice in Utterance Interpretation." *Synthese* 194: 3421–3443.

Peterson, Zoey Leigh. 2017. *Next Year For Sure*. Toronto: Doubleday Canada.

Pierce, C., J. Carew, D. Pierce-Gonzalez, and D. Willis. 1978. "An Experiment in Racism: TV Commercials." In *Television and Education*, edited by C. Pierce, 62–88. Beverly Hills, CA: Sage.

Pohlhaus, Gaile, Jr. 2012. "Relational Knowing and Epistemic Injustice: Toward a Theory of Willful Hermeneutical Ignorance." *Hypatia* 27(4): 715–735.

Roessler, Beate. 2015. "Autonomy, Self-Knowledge, and Oppression." In *Personal Autonomy and Oppression*, edited by Marina Oshana, 68–84. New York: Routledge.

Rogers, Wendy, Catriona Mackenzie, and Susan Dodds. 2012. "Why Bioethics Needs a Concept of Vulnerability." *International Journal of Feminist Approaches to Bioethics* 5: 11–38.

Santiago, John. 2005. "Personal Autonomy: What's Content Got to Do with It?" *Social Theory and Practice* 31(1): 77–104.

Sedgwick, Eve Kosofsky. 1993. *Tendencies*. Durham, NC: Duke University Press.

Sedgwick, Eve Kosofsky. 2000. *A Dialogue on Love*. Boston: Beacon Press.

Sedgwick, Eve Kosofsky. 2003. *Touching Feeling: Affect, Pedagogy, Performativity*. Durham, NC: Duke University Press.

Stoljar, Natalie. 2000. "Autonomy and the Feminist Intuition." In *Relational Autonomy: Feminist Perspectives on Autonomy, Agency, and the Social Self*, edited by Catriona Mackenzie and Natalie Stoljar, 94–111. New York: Oxford University Press.

Stoljar, Natalie. 2014. "Autonomy and Adaptive Preference Formation." In *Autonomy, Oppression, and Gender*, edited by Andrea Veltman and Mark Piper, 227–252. New York: Oxford University Press.

Stoljar, Natalie, and Kristin Voigt. 2022. "Regarding Oneself as an Equal. In *Relational Autonomy and Relational Equality*, edited by Natalie Stoljar and Kristin Voigt, 145–168. New York: Routledge.

Sue, Derald Wing. 2010a. *Microaggressions in Everyday Life: Race, Gender, and Sexual Orientation*. Hoboken: John Wiley & Sons.

Sue, Derald Wing. 2010b. "Microaggressions, Marginality, and Oppression: An Introduction." In *Microagressions and Marginality: Manifestation, Dynamics, and Impact*, edited by Derald Wing Sue, 3–22. Hoboken: John Wiley & Sons.

Sue, Derald Wing, Christina M. Capodilupo, Gina C. Tornin, Jennifer M. Bucceri, Aisha. M. B. Holder, Kevin L. Nadal, and Marta Esquilin. 2007. "Racial Microaggressions in Everyday Life: Implications for Clinical Practice." *American Psychologist* 62: 271–286.

Veltman, Andrea, and Mark Piper, eds. 2014. *Autonomy, Oppression, and Gender*. New York: Oxford University Press.

Watson, Gary. 1975. "Free Agency." *Journal of Philosophy* 72(8): 205–220.

Weir, Allison. 2013. *Identities and Freedom: Feminist Theory between Power and Connection*. Oxford: Oxford University Press.

Westlund, Andrea C. 2009. "Rethinking Relational Autonomy." *Hypatia* 24(4): 26–49.

Wiggins, David. 1987. *Needs, Values, Truth: Essays in the Philosophy of Value*. Oxford: Basil Blackwell.

Wolfe, Katharine. 2016. "Together in Need: Relational Selfhood, Vulnerability to Harm, and Enriching Attachments." *Southern Journal of Philosophy* 54(1): 129–148.

Young, Robert. 1986. *Personal Autonomy: Beyond Negative and Positive Liberty*. London: Croom Helm.

Index

For the benefit of digital users, indexed terms that span two pages (e.g., 52–53) may, on occasion, appear on only one of those pages.

affectation of manner, 77
agential skills, 60–61, 62–63
Ahmed, Sarah, 75–76, 113–14, 115–16, 117–20
Alcoff, Linda Martín, 114–15
Anderson, Joel, 111–12
answerability condition, 100–1, 103–7, 111–13, 117–19
authentic characteristics, 12, 83
authenticity conditions, 5–6, 9–10, 11–12, 30–31, 34, 35–36, 83–85, 89–91, 92, 93–94, 133–34
authentic self, 39
autonomy
   diminished, 28–29, 126–27
   global, 9, 16, 29
   intuitions about, 7–9
   multidimensional concept of, 5–9
   nonautonomous values, 17–18, 27, 41–42, 109–10
   relational, 2–3, 7–8, 17, 100, 121
   securing procedure, 17, 18–19
   social recognition and, 120
   unitary concept of, 7–8
   See also personal autonomy

Babbitt, Susan, 19–20
being believed, 10–11, 41–42, 47–48, 49, 53–54, 55, 128–30
being understood, 10–11, 49–50, 51, 53–54, 55, 129–30
Berlant, Lauren, 84–85, 86–87
bitterness, 12, 85–89, 93, 98–99
broken relations, 133–34

Campbell, Sue, 84–85, 88, 94
causally relational views
   introduction to, 3, 5, 9
   oppression and, 23–24, 122, 124
   self-authorization, 108, 110, 119–20
   self-determination, 15–17, 18–19, 22–24, 25–30, 32

self-expressive activities, 34–38, 41–46, 55–57, 58–59
Charles, Sonya, 20
Christman, John, 90–93
communal competence condition, 10–11, 35–36, 38, 41–55, 56–59, 130
communicative failures, 71–81
communicative needs, 68–71
competence conditions, 10–11, 34, 36
constitutively relational views
   alienation and, 98–99
   alternative dilemmas, 27–29
   authenticity and, 89–93
   authenticity conditions, 83–85, 89–91, 92, 93–94, 133–34
   defined, 3, 35
   emotions and, 85–89
   external world and, 15–16
   introduction to, 83–85
   preemptive criminality, 25
   pro-attitude and, 12, 83, 90–91
   self-determination and, 94–98
   self-governance and, 94–98
   sociopolitical distribution, 85–89, 94–95
   unwanted characteristics, 89–93

damage model of oppression, 9, 17–27, 34
depersonalization conditions, 107
diachronic practical identity, 6–7, 9–10, 22, 30–31, 36, 55, 61, 63–64, 69–70, 81, 121–22, 131
dialogical skills, 34
dignity, 20–21, 107–8, 111–12, 124
diminished autonomy, 28–29, 126–27
displacing relations, 135–36

emotional skills, 34
emotions, 85–89
epistemic exploitation, 53–54
epistemic injustice, 5, 10–11, 35–36, 47–55, 122–23, 129

experiential identity, 116–19
externalism, 29–32

failed relationality, 12, 61, 84–85, 127, 128–30, 132–33, 136
feminism, 2, 18, 73–74, 102
flourishing, human, 19–20, 62–63
Fricker, Miranda, 47–50, 65

global autonomy, 9, 16, 29

happenstance, 38, 40–41, 47–48
hermeneutical ignorance, 50, 52–53, 54–55
hermeneutical inadequacy, 11, 61
hermeneutical injustice, 47–48, 49–50
hermeneutical resources
    communicative failures, 71–81
    communicative needs, 68–71
    failed relationality and, 132–33
    introduction to, 60–61
    nested constitution and, 61, 62–68, 81–82
    practical identity, 60, 61, 63–64, 69–70, 73–74, 77, 79, 81–82
    self-creative activities, 11, 60, 61–63, 67–68, 71, 81–82, 131
    self-understanding and, 81–82
History of Violence (Louis), 11, 61–79, 81–82
homophobia, 71, 72, 77, 87
human flourishing, 19–20, 62–63

identity
    experiential, 116–19
    failed relations and, 132–33
    racialized, 15, 115
    social, 15–18, 22–29, 31–32, 47–48, 62
    superordinate, 9, 16, 25, 30, 32
    See also practical identity
ideological oppression, 19–20
imaginative skills, 36
incarceration, 15–16, 25, 57, 66–67, 86–87, 93, 94–95, 97
instrumentalization of communicative attempt, 70–74, 80, 132–33
interference, 6–7, 16, 24–25, 29–30, 31–32, 97–99, 126–28, 133, 136
internalized oppression, 3–4, 14, 18–19, 20–22, 23
Interpreting the Personal (Campbell), 88
intuitions about autonomy, 7–9

liberal democracies, 2, 112–13, 121
liberatory movements, 2
loneliness, 12, 85–89, 93, 98–99
Louis, Édouard, 11, 61–79, 81–82

Mackenzie, Catriona, 30–31, 67
malrecognition, 13, 100–1, 103–4, 108–13, 115–16, 117, 118, 120, 135
marginalization
    alternative dilemmas of, 27–29
    broken relations and, 133–34
    epistemic injustice, 5, 10–11, 35–36, 47–55, 122–23, 129
    microaggressions, 50–51
    racism, 4, 15, 17, 48–49, 51–52, 53–54, 70–73, 79, 84–85, 86–87, 114–15
    relational absence and, 127, 131–33, 136
    self-authorization and, 103, 109–10, 112–13, 119–20
    self-governance and, 9–11, 33–34, 42–43, 47
    sexism, 4, 15, 17–18, 44–45, 51, 57–58, 115, 129
    social conditions, 2
    systematic constraints of, 47, 48
Meyers, Diana Tietjens, 17–18, 21–22
microaggressions, 50–51
misrecognition, 13, 100–1, 103–4, 108–13, 115–16, 117, 118, 120, 135
motivational systems, 12, 35–37, 47, 85, 95, 97–99, 122, 134
multidimensional concept of autonomy, 5–9

nested constitution, 61, 62–68, 81–82
Next Year for Sure (Peterson), 79–81
nonautonomous values, 17–18, 27, 41–42, 109–10
nonrelational traits, 41–42
normative authority, 6–7, 13, 33n.1, 100, 102–3, 104, 106, 110–13, 117–18, 120, 135

object of desire, 75–76, 114
oppression
    causally relational views and, 23–24, 122, 124
    damage model of, 9, 17–27, 34
    ideological, 19–20
    internalized, 3–4, 14, 18–19, 20–22, 23
    norms of, 3–4, 8–9, 14, 19–20, 22–24, 25–26, 36–37, 62–63, 102–3, 122–24
    social circumstances, 1–2
    sociopolitical spheres of, 15
    superordinate identities, 9, 25, 30, 32
    women's ability and, 21–22, 23–24
oppressive social conditions, 1–2, 3–5, 9–11, 14, 17, 28–29, 32, 33–34, 42–43, 55–56, 84–85, 87, 94–95, 96–98, 101, 121–29, 131, 136
oppressive socialization, 19–20, 23–24
Oshana, Marina, 3–4, 24–25, 30, 35
ownness of life, 15

personal autonomy
    failed relationality and, 12, 61, 84–85, 127, 136
    interrelated aspects of, 6–8
    multidimensional concept of, 8
    overview of, 1–2, 6–7
Peterson, Zoey Leigh, 79–81
Power, Cat, 1
practical identity
    diachronic, 6–7, 9–10, 22, 30–31, 36, 55, 61, 63–64, 69–70, 81, 121–22, 131
    hermeneutical resources, 60, 61, 63–64, 69–70, 73–74, 77, 79, 81–82
    overview of, 9–11
    self-determination and, 30–31
    self-governance and, 36–41
    social recognition, 102, 106, 109, 112–13
pro-attitude, 12, 83, 90–91
proceduralist views, 18–19, 21–22, 26–27

Queer Phenomenology (Ahmed), 75–76, 113–14, 115–16, 117–20

racialized identity, 15, 115
racial profiling, 17, 24–25, 28, 29, 30, 31–32, 48, 122–23
racism, 4, 15, 17, 48–49, 51–52, 53–54, 70–73, 79, 84–85, 86–87, 114–15
rational skills, 34, 36
relational absence, 127, 131–33, 136
relational autonomy, 2–3, 7–8, 17, 100, 121
relational failures. *See* failed relationality
relational property, 38, 40–41, 43–44, 45–47, 56–57, 59

Sedgwick, Eve, 86
self-acceptance, 90–91
self-authorization
    answerability condition, 100–1, 103–7, 111–13, 117–19
    causally relational views, 108, 110, 119–20
    defined, 100
    displacing relations, 135–36
    marginalization and, 103, 109–10, 112–13, 119–20
    normative authority and, 6–7, 13, 33n.1, 100, 102–3, 104, 106, 110–13, 117–18, 120, 135
    overview, 6–8, 13
    social recognition and, 100–4, 106–7, 110–13
self-conception, 60, 74, 93–94n.12, 101, 106, 110–11
self-confidence, 20–21
self-constructive activities, 10–11, 35–38, 41–42, 98–99

self-creative activities, 11, 37–38, 60, 61–63, 67–68, 71, 81–82, 131
self-definition, 6–7, 11, 39, 60–62, 67–70, 74, 81–82, 121, 131–32
self-determination
    alternative dilemmas, 27–29
    broken relations and, 133–34
    causally relational views, 15–17, 18–19, 22–24, 25–30, 32
    constitutively relational views and, 94–98
    damage model and, 9, 17–27, 34
    defined, 57
    externalism and, 29–32
    introduction to, 15–17
    overview of, 6–7, 8–9, 12
    social subordination and, 17–23
self-direction, 39
self-esteem, 3, 18–19, 20, 62–63, 101, 105, 106–12, 120, 135
self-evaluative attitudes
    self-esteem, 3, 18–19, 20, 62–63, 101, 105, 106–12, 120, 135
    self-respect, 3, 18–19, 20, 62–63, 102–3, 105–12, 120, 125–26, 135
    self-trust, 18–19, 20, 62–63, 102–3, 105–12, 120, 125–26, 135
    social recognition and, 101, 102–3, 104–13, 119–20
self-expressive activities, 10–11, 35–38, 41–46, 55–57, 58–59, 60, 122, 128–30
self-governance
    broken relations, 133–34
    communal competence condition, 10–11, 35–36, 38, 41–55, 56–59, 130
    constitutively relational views and, 94–98
    displacing relations, 135–36
    epistemic injustice, 5, 10–11, 35–36, 47–55, 122–23, 129
    failed relationality, 12, 61, 84–85, 127, 128–30, 136
    happenstance and, 38, 40–41, 47–48
    in *History of Violence* (Louis), 11, 61–79, 81–82
    marginalization and, 9–11
    overview of, 6–7, 8–12
    relational absence, 127, 131–33, 136
    relational property, 38, 40–41, 43–44, 45–47, 56–57, 59
    self-expressive activities, 10–11, 35–38, 41–46, 55–57, 58–59, 60, 122, 128–30
    unitary concepts of, 5–8, 30–31
self-knowledge, 34, 55, 63, 65–68, 69–70
self-referential attitudes, 20–21, 28–29

self-reflexive attitudes, 20, 26, 28, 62–63, 101
self-regard, 25–26, 105–6, 107, 122
self-respect, 3, 18–19, 20, 62–63, 102–3, 105–12, 120, 125–26, 135
self-transformation, 67
self-trust, 18–19, 20, 62–63, 102–3, 105–12, 120, 125–26, 135
self-understanding, 11, 34, 36, 81–82
self-worth, 3, 15–16, 20–21, 62–63, 67–68, 135
sexism, 4, 15, 17–18, 44–45, 51, 57–58, 115, 129
social environments, 17, 22, 34, 41, 55–56, 87, 131
social groups, 17, 87–88
social identity, 15–18, 22–29, 31–32, 47–48, 62
social invisibility, 20–21, 107–8
socialization, 3, 5, 14, 17–20, 23–24, 62–63, 87, 122–23
social practices, 2, 8–9, 94–95, 111–12, 126–27, 133–34
social recognition
    answerability condition, 100–1, 103–7, 111–13, 117–19
    autonomy and, 120
    de-authorization practices, 110–20
    displacing relations, 135–36
    importance of, 67
    practical identity, 102, 106, 109, 112–13
    self-authorization and, 100–4, 106–7, 110–13
    self-evaluative attitudes and, 101, 102–3, 104–13, 119–20
social relations, 2–5, 24, 27–28n.16, 28–30, 34–35, 56–57, 67, 86, 106–9, 122–23, 124–25, 128–29, 131
social skills, 34, 36
social subordination, 17–23
sociopolitical distribution, 85–89, 94–95
Stoljar, Natalie, 19–20
substantivist views, 17–18, 19–21
superordinate identities, 9, 16, 25, 30, 32

testimonial injustice, 47–50, 52–53, 54–55, 129
testimonial smothering, 74
trans persons, 25, 30

unhappiness, 39
unitary concept of autonomy, 7–8
unitary concepts, 5–8, 30–31
unwanted characteristics, 89–93

Visible Identities (Alcoff), 114–15
volitional skills, 34, 36

weakly substantive views, 18–19, 101, 102–3, 106, 112–13
Weir, Allison, 1
Wolfe, Katharine, 70
women's agency, 17